M000188790

DON'T SET GOALS...
ACHIEVE THEM!

THE **PRACTICAL GUIDE** FOR **BUILDING MOMENTUM** TO **ACHIEVE YOUR GOALS**

Imowo Enang

PASSIONPRENEUR®
P U B L I S H I N G

Publishing information
Publishing, design, and production facilitated by
Passionpreneur Publishing,
A division of Passionpreneur Organization Pty Ltd,
ABN: 48640637529

www.PassionpreneurPublishing.com
Melbourne, VIC | Australia

Just before you read this book...

D o you ever wonder why nine times out of ten we miss out on our goals?

If we don't approach our goals in the right way, goal-setting may hurt our performance more than help it; this is because of the way our brains respond to challenges.

Do you struggle to achieve your goals?

Don't just set goals – achieve them with the help of this practical guide for building momentum towards achieving your goals! It outlines a foolproof system to accelerate your progress towards sustainable growth and winning at the game of life.

The author shares a tried-and-tested, practical approach for young adults, fresh graduates, and managers forging their exciting paths to success.

Dedication

This book is dedicated to young budding professionals who are seeking their purpose and working to thrive in their niche.

I want you to know you're amazing as you are, and the world awaits your manifestation! See you at the top!!

Acknowledgments

I would like to acknowledge every single person out there who has supported me on my journey, from my dear family to my schoolmates, as well as my colleagues at work, my mentors, and my sponsors.

With you, I keep learning, unlearning, and relearning in the game of life.

About the author

mowo is a business executive for one of the largest global fast-moving consumer goods (FMCG) organizations. He has many years of experience in commercial strategy, operational efficiency, and transformational leadership.

Born and initially raised in Nigeria, Imowo has traveled, worked, and studied in several countries across Africa, Asia, and Europe, giving him unique international insights. Imowo has an MBA and is studying for a doctorate in Strategy. He is a Chartered Manager, a Lean Theory Practitioner, and a Success Principles Coach (Canfield Training Group), as well as a certified Neuro-Linguistic Programming Mind Mastery trainer.

Table of Contents

Introduction

A shocking truth is that people fail to achieve nine out of every ten goals they set. Early goal-setting researchers were surprised to find that setting a goal often hurt people's performance more than it helped. Since then, researchers have found that goal-setting is most helpful for people with a strong drive to achieve. For the many people who don't share this strong drive, setting goals can become an added source of stress, leading to cognitive impairment and lower performance. We also know that goals are most useful for accomplishing routine and relatively simple tasks – the moment we need to innovate, adapt, or learn on the job, setting goals can do more harm than good if we don't approach them in the right way.

But even for routine and repetitive tasks, goal-setting can become counterproductive. At the tail end of the 1970s when the idea of goal-setting and performance feedback was rising in popularity, an automotive plant in Ohio flashed minute-by-minute performance goals on employees' screens as they worked on the production line. Under constant pressure to respond to rapid-fire feedback and meet peak performance goals, the workers protested by going on strike. Since then, studies have confirmed that overly rigorous goal-setting can damage employee engagement and productivity. So why does goal-setting sometimes go so wrong, and how can we get it right?

Problems with goal-setting arise when the brain perceives the goal as a challenge to the existing patterns of thought and action that we use to complete tasks. Neuroscience tells us that any challenge that calls for a radical departure from our usual ways of doing things is processed as a potential threat by the *amygdala*. The amygdala is a part of the limbic system, evolutionarily, one of the oldest systems in the brain. The amygdala's role is to alert us to potential threats to our well-being. It evaluates potential threats and determines whether our memory, decision-making, and emotions will be mobilized to fight and rise aggressively to meet a perceived challenge, or to flee or freeze, shutting down to minimize any damage. When the amygdala perceives a goal to be a threat that is too challenging, we experience a fight or flight response that works against our desire to achieve the goal. The essence of effective goal-setting is to avoid setting off the fight or flight response by setting the bar too high. Instead, we need to formulate goals in a way that will allow us to rise to the challenge.

This goal-setting cookbook gives you a clear step-by-step recipe to achieve the goals you set. You will learn how to establish the systems, processes, and support structures that will guide you to achieve your goals. This simple and practical framework offers you a way to bridge the gap between your goals and your achievement. With this approach, your ability to achieve sustainable growth will significantly improve, helping you to win at the game of life.

If you are a young adult, fresh graduate, or junior to mid-level manager who wants a tried-and-tested approach based on reliable evidence to guide you through the exciting journey of achieving your goals, this book is a great start. While there is a wealth of resources that establish the importance of goal-setting, this book gives you a practical, trusted recipe for achieving your goals.

That's enough preamble – let's get into a bit of my story to kick off the book and get you started!

CHAPTER 1

My Story

*'Success is not final, failure is not fatal: It
is the courage to continue that counts.'*

— Winston Churchill

For a long time, I thought the way you made your bed was the way you had to lie on it – period. Growing up, I believed there was a direct line between a plan and the outcome. And I wasn't alone. On the face of it, it seemed reasonable. You make a plan; achieving your outcome hinges on that plan. But this is only partly true. What happens between making a plan and arriving at the outcome is best described by the iceberg analogy – achieving a goal is just the tip of the iceberg. The work we need to do to get there is the 90% of the iceberg that lies beneath the surface. Most people fail even to see this 90% chunk, and it separates any plan from the eventual outcome. It's no surprise, then, that we see the same ratio for successful goal-setting, with less than 10% of people who set goals achieving them.

I also struggled for some time with my perception of success and my interpretation of what winning meant. I came from a background where 'beginning with the end in mind' – one of the tenets of *the seven habits* – was a way of life and part of an overwhelming focus on achievement. In this approach, everything is about the results (the *what*), not the journey (the *how*). Talking with young people across the globe, I got a similar vibe from their stories. As they begin their careers, many young professionals are indoctrinated into an ideology in which results are everything and nothing else deserves attention. For many of us in this competitive environment, the journey that takes 90% of our time, effort, and opportunity for satisfaction, is not valued.

Over time, I started to realize that this approach was only part of the puzzle I needed to solve to achieve my goals. Of course, results are key, but my perspective changed when I discovered a new way of seeing things. This new lens was Carol Dweck's *'not yet'* approach. I came to understand that the journey itself, and what we see and do while we're on it, will influence and shape our perceptions of success. The journey must be part of what we understand as winning. From this new perspective, I reorganized my thinking to focus more on *progress* along the way, rather than the simple point in time represented by *success*. For me, focusing on progress is part of creating *momentum* from a plan toward a final goal. I focus on the *not yet* phase, the steps along the way before we reach the goal – the place where we spend most of our time and effort.

This change of perspective disrupted my usual approach to completing daily or weekly tasks and allowed me to see things in a more positive light. Of course, this was not a step away from hard work. My experience confirmed the 'power of *and*' by combining working hard *and* working smart. With this new approach, my efficiency took off to reach previously unimaginable levels. I do almost all the things I love and enjoy and still excel in every endeavor. As a team leader with several years of management and leadership experience under my belt, I have learned first-hand that these things make the most difference for success. In the long term, these vital actions will bring us much greater value than they cost and result in a positive benefit/cost ratio across our endeavors. These principles have worked for me and now I want to share them with people who walk in the same shoes and help them raise the bar on what they can do.

This approach cuts across all age brackets, and these simple principles have been applied by many phenomenal individuals to drive them to win at the game of life. I have tested these systems and methods with over a hundred people who have had similar struggles to mine.

These volunteers gave valuable feedback, which I have incorporated into the frameworks you will see.

In this book I break the method down into simple, practical steps that are an easy-to-follow blueprint for success. Central to this approach is a *modus operandi* that will become automatic with practice. We can train our minds to learn, retain, and apply this process daily to make incremental progress in our numerous endeavors.

First, the *Disrupt Your Mind section* provides tools to guide you to a crystal-clear purpose. Using these tools, you will identify your purpose by understanding what connects your passions, your principles, and your skill sets.

Next, you will learn how to *Disrupt Your Methods* by *creating powerful connections*. Have you ever wondered why what we fear the most often comes true? This is due to the power of mental imagery to attract the future. We can create and build, or destroy and tear down, with our creative human abilities. But to achieve our goals, we need to harness our creative abilities and connect them to our passions and goals. What I share in this book is how to use synchronicities as tools to establish the right connections, harness the laws of attraction, and leverage the resources and capabilities that will allow you to increase your outputs with fewer inputs.

With these tools, you can disrupt your existing methods to build complementary solutions, as in the Lego system, where building blocks are shaped and positioned to enable you to build your goals and deliver on them.

Finally, you will learn how to *Execute with Excellence.* That means executing your plans *via consistency* within the *framework of continuous improvement.* A.G. Lafley, a former CEO of Procter & Gamble, one of the biggest fast-moving consumer goods (FMCG) players in history, famously said that execution is the *ONLY* strategy the customer sees. Lafley meant that without the right execution, all the background work, ideation, conceptualization, and design are redundant. What matters is carrying out the plan. Even after we find clarity of purpose and establish the right connections, we will find ourselves back at the starting line if we don't drive consistent execution.

These three disruptions, Mind, Methods and Execution, will enable you to achieve incremental improvements along your journey to achieving your final goals.

Before going any further, we must look at the big picture. So, walk with me on this exciting journey!

CHAPTER 2

Big picture – Go for gold and not for goals

'A staggering 92% of people who set goals failed to achieve them.'

— Scranton University

Set up the right systems, processes and support structures

How many times have you set goals in your life? And how many times have you achieved them? They say that actions speak louder than words and that's why Carl Gustav Jung, Swiss psychoanalyst and the founder of analytical psychology, said, 'You are what you do, not what you say you'll do.'

Execution is the biggest barrier most of us face to making our goals a reality. So, if goal-setting has only 8% success, is there a proven formula for achieving the goals we set?

In this chapter, you will see goal-setting in a different light as you explore success through the lens of progress vs. point-in-time achievements. This will happen as we shift our mindset from the legacy goal-setting focus to goal achievement criteria. Finally, you will observe the Triple C approach, comprising *clarity of purpose, creating connections, and consistency in delivery*, as the guiding light to transition your goals into reality

The issue with just goal-setting

For a long time, I thought setting goals was the ultimate driver of achieving goals. I learned how to set SMART goals – *Specific, Measurable, Achievable, Realistic, and Time-bound goals* – and then SMAC goals – *Specific, Measurable, Achievable, and Concise*. I learned systems that suggested I 'raise the bar as high as possible when setting [my] goals'; that is, in the words of you Norman Vincent Peale, 'shoot for the moon because if you fall short, you will land amongst the stars.' Other systems proclaimed the merits of making a goal as concrete, simple, and realistic as possible so that once it has been achieved you can reach for the next goal. The idea that connects these lines of thought is that we have to set the bar somewhere, whether high or low, and aim to get over that bar!

Let's look more closely at SMART and SMAC goal-setting. The philosophy guiding them both is to set out and quantify what you must do to achieve your ultimate goal. By setting clear and measurable goals you will create realistic expectations about what *success* will look like. It is vital to focus on clearly defined and measurable targets to clearly define success. That is how we measure performance in the corporate world, in academia, and in many other endeavors, right? But we must also measure and value our efforts along the way to success and our incremental progress.

In many approaches, achieving the goal is the only success. If I take that approach and set myself the target of running one kilometer in six minutes, I will not be successful until I beat the six-minute barrier. But success is a journey, and a potent attitude to finding success is being the best you can be based on your current resources and environment. Success should be seen as unfolding over time, rather than existing only at the one point when the final goal is achieved. We need to focus on driving momentum, rather than focusing only on the endpoint. Here, we need to consider two important points:

1. It's the journey that matters. Anyone can share the 'what' of goal-setting. Setting a target is the

easiest part of the endeavor, but walking the path toward the goal is the real challenge.

2. We need to appreciate small incremental wins along the path to success. Studies have shown that individuals achieve greater success in executing their goals when they pursue a sequence of step-by-step targets than when they set one big target without planning specific steps to take along the way. This is the strength of focusing on the process rather than the outcome.

Let's take one of my goals as an example. I aimed to run 42 kilometers, effectively a marathon, every month. This was a big dream, and many of you may be able to relate to my failure to achieve it because it was just too big and I had no structure for getting there. Goal-setting wasn't the issue, executing my goal was the problem! Ten years later, I decided to try to reach my goal by taking small, measurable steps. I started running one kilometer every other day. By achieving this smaller goal, I built up the motivation to run two kilometers every three days. Next, somehow, I was running four kilometers twice a week, until I could increase the distance to five kilometers twice a week. At that point, I was running ten kilometers a week and forty kilometers every four weeks – more or less a marathon every month. I had achieved my goal!

The best path to success is to divide your ultimate goal into a series of smaller daily or weekly goals that are clear and specific and will be easier to accomplish. Recent research has shown that as humans, we perform better when we focus on incremental change – small step-by-step improvements – than when we focus on big overall changes. This phenomenon is explained by the *theory of marginal gains* and has been described by the *1% principle* coined by Sir Dave Brailsford. From fitness goals to professional goals, in education, business, and other fields, people are finding that a consistent 1% change makes a big difference over time. Focusing on small incremental changes will lead to significant *transformational* change on a more sustainable basis than aiming to achieve a bigger change in one giant step.

The *theory of marginal gains* goes back to the Beijing Olympics in 2008, and with the London Olympics in 2012 we saw the magnitude of this game-changing approach to goal achievement. Sir Dave Brailsford took over as head of British cycling in 2002 and, in 2008, led his team at the Beijing Olympics to deliver its best performance in 76 years. He applied the theory of marginal gains to take the ailing British Cycling Federation from just two bronze medals at the 1984 Atlanta Olympics to an amazing seven gold medals in Beijing in 2008, and then on to a remarkable tally of eight gold, two silver, and two bronze at the London Games in 2012. The team went on to win a further six gold, four silver, and one bronze at the Rio Olympic Games in 2016.

The theory of marginal improvement via the 1% rule is summed up by the idea of *continuous improvement*. Brailsford concentrated on driving *small improvements every day*, everywhere, and anywhere, one step at a time. The 1% principle led to significant breakthrough improvements for his team.

Roadmap for achieving your goals

This book gives you a road map for achieving your goals using a proven model. The model will help you gain clarity about your purpose and enable you to establish the connections needed to achieve it through visualizing and executing your goals with an unwavering focus on the process. The book will show you how to integrate your purpose and your day-to-day actions to build momentum and turn a continuous improvement approach into a habit. You will find out how to leverage the elements that drive continuous improvement and practice the habits that will allow you to achieve your ultimate goal, all while staying focused on the journey.

The roadmap – clarity of purpose, connections, and consistency

1. Clarity of purpose

Thomas Leonard said, 'clarity affords focus.' Clarity is the guiding light to align effort with purpose. Everything is in vain unless you have a clear purpose. Purpose is critical for driving meaning into what we do every day, while clarity helps us to crystalize our expectations through visualization. If a picture is worth a thousand words, visualization is a powerful tool to unlock more drive, purpose, and meaning in all that we do.

Visualization is part of a broader concept of *mental imagery*. We produce mental imagery using inputs from our five senses, creating a multi-faceted quasi-reality that mimics the real world. Mental imagery is a form of mental modeling through which we imagine potential futures, and these imagined futures enables us create our future reality. In 2019, 19-year-old Canadian tennis player Bianca Andreescu defeated the world champion, Serena Williams, at the US Open – an incredible achievement. During post-match interviews, Andreescu revealed that during her adolescent years of training and competing, she would close her eyes and 'envision [herself] winning the US Open one day against Williams...' She said, 'I guess visualizations really work!' The daily practice of tapping into mental imagery to experience goal achievement can accelerate those dreams into reality.

Mental imagery has been used successfully for many decades in the sporting world and its influence has spread to other areas of endeavor, including business and education. Sport is replete with examples of athletes using mental imagery to break barriers and set new world records. Mental imagery helps athletes and players persist and find the drive they need to practice for thousands of hours to stay in top form and prepare for major events. These athletes repeatedly imagine what they want to achieve and attract success in real-time. This effective mental imagery technique is free and fun for anyone to use!

Olympic swimmer, Michael Phelps, said, 'One of the things that has been good for me, I think, besides training, has been my sort of mental preparation.' Kathleen Ledecky, a competitive US 400-, 800-, and 1500-meter freestyle swimmer who has won five Olympic gold medals and fifteen world championship gold medals, making her the most awarded female swimmer in history, said, 'I have my goals and I visualize things to help me achieve those goals. I know what my stroke should feel like at different parts of the race, and I can just kind of picture that in my mind.'

Outside the sporting realm, Oprah has acknowledged that visualization, and in a broader sense, mental imagery, was instrumental in securing her celebrated role in *The Color Purple.* Oprah creates vision boards that include images to help her visualize specific outcomes: 'I have been using visualization to help me achieve my goals since I was a little girl. My latest vision board, which is a scrapbook, was created two years ago when my business was facing near-impossible odds of survival.' Further evidence of the unique role of visualization in Oprah's journey to stardom can be seen when she said, 'I visualized profits, success, and satisfaction – I even cut out the cover of *Inc.* magazine and pasted my face on it. At the time it seemed almost inconceivable that any of it would happen, and yet a short eighteen months later that's exactly where I found myself.'

Renowned author and globally recognized success coach, Jack Canfield, identified four key benefits of visualization (part of mental imagery) for achieving goals:

1. Visualization *stimulates your creative subconscious*. Once this happens, creativity becomes the norm and increases your mental ability and creative capacity.
2. Visualization *increases mental alertness*. You will become more mentally alert and expand the inner resources that are critical for achieving your goals.

3. Visualization activates the *law of attraction*. This means the people, activity systems, and environments you need to achieve your goals will be more easily perceived and attracted to you.

4. With these effects, you gain more confidence in yourself and your creative abilities and will more strongly believe that you're well-positioned to achieve your goals.

2. Higher-order mental imagery – putting it down on paper

By writing down your goals, you can visualize them more easily. Perhaps as a student you noticed that summarizing lectures and writing down the main points helps you to visualize and recall the experience of learning better than just reading or listening to the same information. As a young high school dude, I would summarize the key points on small pieces of paper I could carry around. Essentially, what we see influences how we act – when we put ideas down on paper, we connect the creative and imaginative parts of our brains with the logical, analytical parts that are involved in planning and executing our plans.

Dr. Gill Matthew, a psychology professor at the Dominican University in California, surveyed almost 270 people and discovered that we are 42% more likely to achieve our goals if we write them down. By recording a visualized activity in ink, we strengthen connections in the brain and lay down the foundation for execution. The actions involved in the visualized outcome are distilled and processed in the brain's activity centers, as driven by the act of writing them down.

If setting our vision down in ink is the second level of mental imagery, are there real-life examples to validate this? For sure! Many celebrities and top performers have used this principle to achieve amazing results. Jim Carrey wrote himself a $10 million check for 'acting services rendered' and postdated it to ten years after the day he wrote it. Ten years later, he earned a $10 million check for his role in the classic movie *Dumb and Dumber*. Some may call it luck or coincidence, but it can't be denied that Carrey elevated mental imagery to the next level by writing down what he had visualized. Carrey activated the law of attraction and got what he aimed for!

How about Bruce Lee, super-famous martial artist and star of popular movies? In the late 1960s, he wrote a letter to himself titled *My Definite Chief Aim:*

> *I Bruce Lee will be the first highest paid Oriental superstar in the United States. In return I will give the most exciting performances and render the best of quality in the capacity of an actor.*

Starting 1970 I will achieve world fame and from then onward till the end of 1980 I will have in my possession $10,000,000. I will live the way I please and achieve inner harmony and happiness. Bruce Lee, Jan 1969.

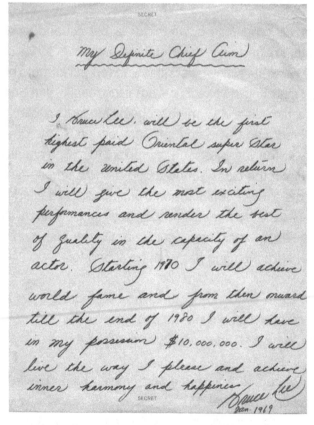

"MY DEFINITE CHIEF AIM": BRUCE LEE'S LETTER TO HIMSELF

His note was written in 1969 and by the time Bruce Lee had turned 32, he had achieved these lofty career goals and more. Again, some may attribute this to some unusual stroke of luck...however, as you may have observed, just like Jim Carrey, Bruce Lee used the second-order of mental imagery to prompt himself to execute his goals: he first deliberated on his goals via visualization and then further articulated the same by distilling them down on paper! Same principle, different individuals – similar outcomes! Sir John Hargrave, the author of *Mind Hacking*, aptly summed up the effectiveness of writing down mental imagery to activate your goals: 'Until it's on paper, it's vapor.'

3. Creating Connections

Establishing the right connections hinges on the fact that the whole is greater than the sum of its parts. Or, according to a popular African proverb, 'If you want to go fast, go alone, but if you want to go far, go together.' We can't achieve our overall vision by walking alone. We need to build scale, integrate resources, complement our gaps, and leverage opportunities to strengthen our chances of progressing.

When we establish these elements, we activate the law of attraction via synchronicity. Synchronicity, coined by Carl Dug, is when events that may originally be unrelated occur at the same time and create a meaningful coincidence. Synchronicity provides an opportunity for creative connections through strong attractions between what we believe and what we perceive around us. Synchronicity with other people and events is key to aligning our behavior and actions with our purpose, and it also allows us the opportunity to focus clearly on the path to success rather than the point of ultimate success alone.

We see synchronicity in our surroundings – with trees in their relative movements and growth patterns, fishes as they move together in groups, and birds as they collectively chirp into a song as if pre-planned. There is a popular saying that goes, 'If you fail to prepare, then you're preparing to fail.' Similarly, we hear that chance favors those who prepare. Many people encounter opportunities, but the factor differentiating those who succeed from those who don't is their level of preparedness. Preparedness attracts the 'good fortune' most people assume was bestowed by chance but, in reality, was gained through hard work and forethought.

Have you ever noticed that when you become good at a skill, the achievement often seems to have come by luck? It's not luck – it's you, improving through practice, more practice, and even more practice. Here, the *ten-thousand-hour rule* is a good guide. Promoted by Malcolm Gladwell in *Outliers,* the ten-thousand-hour rule describes the idea that enough practice of a skill will make an expert of anyone. More recent research has shown that success often requires more than practice, and for many skills, achieving expertise may depend on a person's underlying capacities. But for many other skills, as Gladwell said, 'ten thousand hours is the magic number of greatness.'

4. Consistency in delivery

I'll remind you of what A.G. Lafley, former CEO of Procter & Gamble said: 'Execution is the ONLY strategy the customer sees.' This means that without effective execution, even the greatest background work, ideation, conceptualization, and design will come to nothing. After developing clarity of purpose and connecting with others, we are back at the starting line if we don't drive consistent execution.

Focus on the process, not the outcome

The most sustainable way to drive consistency is to focus on the process rather than the outcome. As we have learned, this stems from the need not to just set goals, but to build momentum to achieve them. In project management, *quality assurance* is about providing confidence that quality requirements will be fulfilled. To provide confidence, the processes of execution must be qualified to ensure the outcome meets the brief or is quality compliant. In the same vein, during goal-setting, once we fix the processes the outcome is invariably achieved.

Amy Cuddy, a renowned Harvard-trained psychologist, claims that the average person will find more success if they shoot for *just down the block* instead of shooting for the moon. This is another way to say that we must focus more on the process or the journey toward our bigger goals, than on the outcome. If your goal is to lose ten kilos, you can't achieve it overnight. Instead, your best option is to divide your ultimate goal into a series of smaller daily or weekly goals that will be easier to accomplish. According to Cuddy, 'lots of research is showing us that we do much better when we focus on incremental change, on little bits of improvement,' and that 'the biggest mistake a lot of people make in setting goals for themselves is that they focus only on the outcome, not the process.'

James Clear, *New York Times* best-selling author of *Atomic Habits*, put it this way, 'Every Olympian wants to win a gold medal. Every candidate wants to get the job. And if successful and unsuccessful people share the same goals, then the goal cannot be what differentiates the winners from the losers.' To create and achieve success in completing these little bits of improvement, we need to create systems that set us up for success.

What did we learn?

This chapter de-mystified perennial misconceptions about setting goals and helped us understand the need to accelerate momentum toward achieving our goals through visualizing success and focusing on the process rather than the outcome.

We looked at what is involved in shifting our mindset from goal-setting to goal achievement, touching on misconceptions that might hold us back and establishing the reasons why adopting a disruptive approach to goal achievement is the new approach.

Finally, we outlined a clear roadmap for executing incremental change using the Triple C approach of *clarity of purpose, creating connections, and consistency in delivery.*

The next chapter will take us through the journey of gaining *clarity of purpose* to help us understand our big *why* and set the stage for other elements we need to achieve our goals through building momentum.

CHAPTER 3

Clarity of purpose –
The big 'why'

*"'What am I living for?" and "What am I
dying for?" are the same question.'*

— Margaret Atwood

What is your mission on the planet? Why were you born? There is something unique about every person. Our fingerprints are unique; no one across the entire globe has the same set of ridges and lines as you. Even the most identical of twins have different fingerprints. Each person also has a unique contribution to make to the human experience, unique pathways to follow, and unique challenges to face as we set out on life's journey. Until we make a difference, we are not fulfilling our potential.

But how do we work toward making a valuable contribution? It all lies in our purpose!

By the end of this chapter, you will understand that purpose is the epicenter of everything we do. You will see why having a clear purpose makes all the difference, by articulating the value of our unique contribution and outlining the roadmap to achieve our goals. Purpose acts as a lighthouse to bring us back on track when we stray.

What drives you?

Think about a time when you did something that would make a positive impact, not just on you but on others. Can you remember a time when you were generous to someone and felt more excited when they received the gift than they did themselves? These moments leave us with a sense of fulfillment and contentment. I vividly recall being approached by a friend's mother at my graduation. She said, 'I just want to thank you for being an inspiration to my son in his studies. He always talked about how you supported him, especially in your finals.' She went on to say, 'I know your parents will be very proud of you. God bless you indeed.' I was surprised and close to tears. The moment was touching and made me feel I had contributed something valuable.

Our lives become truly meaningful when we have a positive impact on others, when we go beyond working and living for ourselves alone. Our contributions are magnified when we give to others. The more we grow, the more we should tailor our passions to inspire others. This larger-than-life effect is synonymous with what Shawn Baldwin, Senior Vice President at Walmart Stores, described: 'As leaders we have the opportunity to bring people together to do something bigger than they are as individuals.'

Tony Robbins perfectly explained how 'the secret to living is giving.' This phrase has resonated with me for a long time and was further clarified by Dr. Wayne Dyer when he explained how serotonin is released in the brain when we give to others. Serotonin is a neurotransmitter produced in the brain that chemically rewards us for behavior that is adaptive and good for our wellbeing. At the same time, it relieves sadness and depression – it's called the 'feel-good hormone.' Serotonin is released during acts of kindness, especially giving. Serotonin isn't released only in the person giving, but also in the recipient and in observers. Giving to others brings manifold positive effects in social groups and directly connects with our purpose. We each want to feel good. We feel even better when others feel good, too. In this way, giving to others becomes a central part of our true purpose.

But how do we find and understand our purpose, let alone gain clarity of purpose?

Finding your sense of purpose

For many decades, psychologists have sought to understand how human goals have evolved through history
and within the human lifespan. We know that long-term
goals that activate a sense of purpose in people change
their lives for the better and give them greater meaning.

You might think that the only purpose that counts is the
pursuit of *Big Hairy Audacious Goals (BHAG),* such as
finding a cure for serious disease, setting up an NGO
(non-governmental organization), or launching an organization or business to find solutions to perennial social
problems. But people gain meaning from a more life-
sized purpose, such as teaching kids how to read and
write or crafting a small start-up business that creates
value in its own way. As long as your endeavor has a
positive impact on people other than just yourself, it
can link into your longer-term purpose.

As individuals, our purpose does not need to be tied
exclusively to the special talents or gifts we hold. Our
talent may very well be just the starting point. No matter how amazingly gifted one is, if it isn't put to use, the
gift will wane. Rather than finding your purpose in your
talents and abilities, you can work on establishing it

through passion and work. You can nurture your goal over time, and it will connect your values, principles, and intentions to contribute to humanity.

Five critical questions that help us unwrap our sense of purpose

1. What is the burden that you feel you are uniquely suited to help lift?
2. What are your unique skills? Where do you out-perform all others?
3. What leads you to feel most fulfilled whenever you do it?
4. What do others appreciate most about you?
5. What constitutes your overall disposition when you're operating at your peak?

Gathering information by reading widely and putting together your own experiences in writing can help you achieve more clarity in your goals and forge a sense of purpose. Again, it is true that the more you work on your passion, the clearer your purpose will become. Your passion will get clearer with greater focus. Your passion may lead you to your purpose, but they remain fundamentally different points on the divide.

Purpose demystified

Our *purpose* as humans is the sum or aggregate of our *passion* (which is essentially what we aim to achieve with our time), our *principles* (that govern our activity), and the *skills* we have amassed through our talent and our learning.

Purpose is '*Y*' we exist, and so our *Purpose Equation* is:

Purpose [Y] = Passion [X] * Principles [C] * Skills [S]
or, Y= XCS

Passion

It's amazing how people's priorities change when it's time for the Premier League, or maybe that Netflix series we are unrepentantly addicted to! The reason we get goosebumps or an adrenaline rush when we're watching our favorite team is our passion for it. Take it one step further and imagine you're an actor and not just a spectator. Just imagine for a minute that you're at the epicenter of a World Cup soccer match, you're Cristiano Ronaldo. The odds are that you're mega-passionate about what you do, right? According to a basic principle of motivation, the more passionate you are about an activity, the more skilled you become at it and, in turn, the more passionate you become. This cycle explains why building skill usually translates to higher motivation. There is a direct relationship between attaining skills to improve our capabilities and increasing levels of both motivation and competence.

Carol Dweck developed the notion of the *growth mindset*, whereby people who believe their skills and capabilities can grow tend to achieve more than people who believe their skills and capabilities are fixed. People with a fixed mindset do not rise to meet a challenge that is beyond their existing skillset. Unwrapping Carol Dweck's notion of the *growth mindset*, we can see similarities between passion and growth. Like skills, interests and passion are not fixed. Through the exertion of effort and hard work, we also stimulate growth and development in our interests and passions.

But while passion is a key input to purpose, it is not purpose itself. Passion evokes emotions that make us feel good about ourselves and the activity we're engaging in; this pleasure is an internal incentive that fuels our motivation to continue pursuing those activities. Passion answers the *what* question, while purpose provides the *why* and is the key driver of what we do. Passion feeds into purpose but is more short-term, transient, and observable. In contrast, purpose is more long-term and internal.

However, passion can be the lighthouse that points us to our purpose. As T.D. Jakes puts it, 'If you can't figure out your purpose, figure out your passion. For your passion will lead you right into your purpose.'

Principles

Our principles are like a guiding compass – they help us navigate. They set us in the right direction and prevent us from going astray. Generally, principles ensure that we stay in line with our expectations for ourselves. You might ask, why do we need these rules? Well, your guess is as good as mine. The nice-to-have freedom of choice in *what we want to do* may not always match *what we need to do*.

We all know it can feel kind of nice to stay home from school and relax rather than hop onto a bus and go through the stress of getting to class or, in these days of online classes, logging in to the online classroom. It also feels nice to eat an entire pack of chocolates and indulge in that ice cream and pastry combo, even when we know we've had a bit too much already. Or perhaps we'd like to test our new car to see if it can accelerate as quickly as the manual claims, even if it means breaking the speed limits. There are many things we *want to do* but don't *need to do*, and many other things that we *don't want to do* but *need to do*. It feels like we're in a constant war of will!

That's when our principles step in. Our principles save us from ourselves. They are the tools that allow us to act according to our value system and stay true to our moral standards. But more important is the execution of our principles. Moral principles should be executed in the same way as scientific principles – as broad guidelines that describe fundamental truths about the consequences of different actions. When we approach principles this way, we can see why we need to uphold fundamental truths for ourselves.

Skills

Talent, they say, is overrated. Talent puts you head and shoulders above those who are less talented at the same endeavor, right? Talent almost seems like a cheat sheet or a head-start in the race. But that's not the case! Wayne Butler summarized it nicely, 'Everyone has their own talents, it's up to you to see what you can actually do!' Einstein insisted that genius is 1% talent and 99% percent hard work. If intrinsic talent is not sharpened with time and hard work into skill, you will lose the head start.

Talent is simple. It comes naturally through imbued gifts. That's it! It's great to have talents, as they are a bonus, a step up. But no matter how talented you are, your talent will fail you if you don't develop it into *skills*. This explains why some people start amazingly well but cannot sustain a high level of 'greatness' over time – and why some people start from *zero* and accelerate each and every day to *hero*.

We build skills through rigorously and diligently driving improvement in our crafts. The ten-thousand-hour rule popularized by Malcolm Gladwell is a great model of how skills can be built. By plugging in up to ten thousand hours in many activities, a fair level of mastery is achieved. This is the generation of skill. Skill is validated talent on steroids. Skill is also usually on a continuous improvement cycle, which is also why maintaining skill can be so brutal. Basically, if you don't use it, you lose it!

The alignment of *passion, principles, and skills* is the true indicator of your *purpose* and will enable you to achieve *clarity* in your purpose.

Our purpose is the driving force that propels us to live beyond just existing

Surveys from a variety of organizations reveal that employees have a burning desire to be connected to something bigger than the routine work they do. People want to connect with the *Big Hairy Audacious Goals (BHAG)* of their company – its mission and vision. Employees want to be engaged in meaningful work, critical projects that enable them not only to connect with the core goals of the company but also to grow through coaching, mentoring, and capacity building.

Once you align people with meaningful goals and provide work environments that afford them the flexibility to act creatively, there's nothing they can't achieve. In these optimal conditions, people develop passion for their roles, and this passion becomes aligned with their growing skills and underlying principles to deliver amazing results by tapping into the vehicle of their purpose.

Research by the Corporate Leadership Council has shown that fewer than 20% of senior leaders are *Talent Champions*. Talent Champions are leaders who drive excellence in delivering on their tasks not only through high-level personal commitment but through building the capabilities and skills of employees. Talent Champions' teams demonstrate higher results, engagement, and retention. Championing talent is a significant opportunity to connect people's passions and talents to their roles, contributions, and aspirations; leaders often leave passions and talents untapped. Championing the skills and capabilities of employees is a truly rewarding journey for senior managers, leaders, and members of the executive.

We have seen how the alignment of passion, principles, and skills leads to the development of clarity of purpose to make a difference. The diagram on the next page consolidates what you have learned so far in understanding what your true purpose might be.

1] Disrupt your Mind- *Clarity of Purpose*

'What am I living for?' and 'What am I dying for?' are the same question. —Margaret Atwood

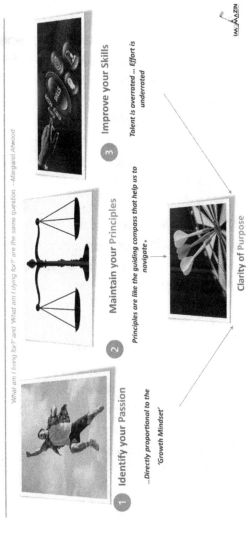

Identify your Passion

...Directly proportional to the 'Growth Mindset'

Maintain your Principles

Principles are like the guiding compass that help us to navigate.

Improve your Skills

Talent is overrated ... Effort is underrated

Clarity of Purpose

ADAPTED FROM "3 STEPS TO ACHIEVING YOUR GOALS". SOURCE: IMOWO ENANG

What did we learn?

We started this chapter by probing deeper to understand who we are and what we bring to the world and our communities as social individuals. This is a top priority for all of us and is generally the starting point in our overall journey to achieving our goals. We explored the concept of having a sense of purpose and uncovered ways to identify that sense of purpose.

We continued to unwrap purpose as an outcome of pursuing our passion – a renewable energy that is generated when we align our interests with a growth mindset, an expanding skillset, and principles that keep us to our moral obligations.

What's next?

Let's look at some recommended actions for putting the information shared so far into practice. These exercises will bring your learning to life and help you define and clarify your purpose, or recalibrate your purpose if you have already found it.

Exercise I

Answer these questions to guide your understanding of your clarity of purpose:

- Do I truly believe in myself? [Insert your name] – *Everything starts with you!*
- Can I talk for two minutes with anyone about my vision and how this will create value for others? *If you can't communicate it, it is not yet clear!*
- Is there anyone I have read or heard about that had a similar vision? *No idea or endeavor is original; there's nothing new under that sun. The fact that you can connect it somehow with someone or something means it's relevant and applicable.*
- Have I broken down the structure of my purpose into smaller actionable parts? *This makes things achievable.*
- Am I aware of the risks of acting against my purpose? *We must understand the factors that work counter to our purpose.*
- Do I have a risk mitigation plan to address these risks? *We must develop mitigating solutions to risks and plan proactively to manage them.*
- Will I truly make a difference? Am I making someone's life better? *If not, you're wasting your time. Your life will only become better by making others' lives better.*

Exercise II

Identify your purpose

Next, let's try to understand our purpose by asking ourselves a few questions:

Questions:

- What pursuits would inspire and give meaning to you?
- What impact would you like to make on others?
- Is there a way to match and merge the first two questions into one statement?

Assess your passion

Questions:

- What do I think about most?
- What gives me energy and makes me come alive?
- What are the things I do or have done in the past that have evolved to shape my purpose?
- How do my answers connect to my interests and dreams from my early days?

Understand your principles

List your principles and ask yourself the questions below.

Questions:

- What do I or other people identify as my moral standards?
- What protects me from crossing boundaries I know will impact my moral obligations?

Focus on your skillsets

Questions:

- What are the unique talents you have harnessed over the years that give you a competitive edge?
- Can you list the skillsets you have acquired in the course of your work, study, and interaction with people that have now set you apart from the crowd?
- Can you calibrate the level of your skills in terms of your stage of mastery (basic, advanced, mastery)?

Now, we will run one last activity, Exercise III. This will lead you to put your purpose into a strong visual representation of your internal desires. You will unwrap mental imagery and reveal its potency to support your purpose and enable you to make the giant leap to achieving your goals.

Exercise III

This framework is a self-diagnostic tool that can help you identify your purpose. Starting from 'Talents' at the top of the diagram, answer the questions and follow the path directed by your answers.

In the empty framework below, insert your answers to the questions in the self-diagnostic tool.

Purpose Flow Questions: Connecting your Passion | Principles | Skills & Talents

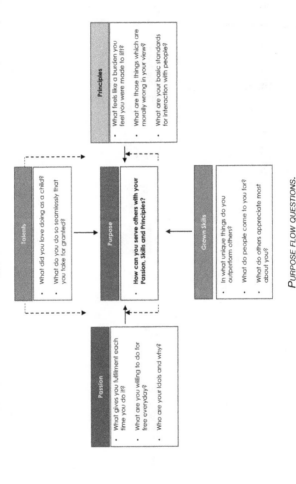

Principles
- What feels like a burden you feel you were made to lift?
- What are those things which are morally wrong in your view?
- What are your basic standards for interaction with people?

Talents
- What did you love doing as a child?
- What do you do so seamlessly that you take for granted?

Purpose
- **How can you serve others with your Passion, Skills and Principles?**

Grown Skills
- In what unique things do you outperform others?
- What do people come to you for?
- What do others appreciate most about you?

Passion
- What gives you fulfilment each time you do it?
- What are you willing to do for free everyday?
- Who are your Idols and why?

PURPOSE FLOW QUESTIONS.

Purpose Flow Template: Connecting your Passion | Principles | Skills & Talents

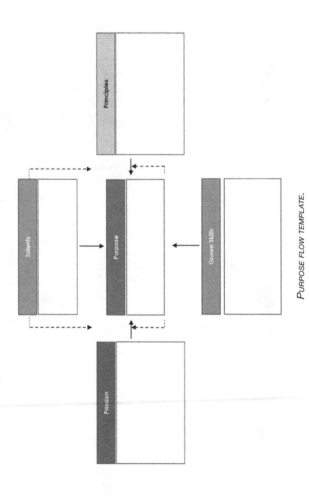

PURPOSE FLOW TEMPLATE.

CHAPTER 4

The Power of Mental Imagery

*'A picture is worth more than
a thousand words.'*

— Chinese proverb

Activating visualization and more

One of the major roadblocks faced by researchers and business leaders is the need to present complex insights in a way that is both meaningful and easy to understand. Constructing a building involves putting thousands of pieces of information together in a complex design and then bringing this to life. Imagine a building design without drawings!

Have you ever wondered why what we fear the most is sometimes what happens? This can occur because of the power of mental imagery. We can create and build, or tear down and destroy, within our human capacity for creativity.

This chapter will explain the mystery behind the creative power of mental imagery. You will see how we can design new things from nothing by visually coupling elements together, using a combination of our five senses and deliberating on them until an original design emerges. You will also understand why our cognitive systems interpret both mental imagery and reality in similar ways. Finally, you will see examples of people like you and me who have transformed their lives with this 'capability,' and you will see easy ways to apply it as well.

Mental imagery

Think about a time when you wanted something so badly that you began to see it more and more in your thoughts until it began to play in your mind like a movie. Then, when it eventually happened, it was as if it had happened before. Or *had* it happened before? It happened in your mind and then happened again in the real world. A repeat!

The concept of mental imagery was introduced when researchers uncovered the importance of visual representation in our everyday lives. People often refer to visualization as mental imagery, but visualization is just one part of mental imagery. Mental imagery incorporates impressions captured by all our five senses. The *Cambridge Dictionary* suggests that 'mental imagery is a trial run of what it would be like to experience such a perception.'

We dive deeply into the imagination and connect our impressions to the power of mental imagery, which is such a potent tool that it magnifies our impressions and creates a rich future out of a bleak present.

When I was ten years old and a couple of months away from finishing grade six, I was so excited to be graduating and progressing to high school that I dreamed about the graduation event. I saw the entire event, from the clothes I would wear to having my achievements in mathematics acknowledged, to the food served during the graduation celebration. I dreamed of this scene every day and each time it became clearer. When my graduation day came, I was amazed when it unfolded exactly as I had imagined. At the time, I believed this was simply a nice coincidence. But today I know better.

Mental imagery has been scientifically confirmed as a potent way to create the future. Research has mapped the mechanics of visualization when we create mental imagery, and the power of imagination to visualize the future. Many examples of the influence of visualization have been identified. The power of mental imagery has long been embraced by religions, and now we have developed innovative *virtual reality* tools that are based on the premise of visualization.

Understanding the effects of mental imagery can magnify your impact. Mental imagery is a potent tool in business, career-building, education, sports, religion, and every facet of human endeavor, as it unleashes our creative human capabilities. For many centuries, it has been the catalyst that thinkers have deployed to implement their designs.

How does mental imagery work?

Mental imagery including visualization stimulates the creative capabilities of the mind and incentivizes creativity by tapping into the things that appeal most to the individual. But its power doesn't stop there. Visualization incentivizes creativity steadily and surely until it stretches our usual level of performance. Then, visualization translates creativity into the day-to-day activities of that individual.

Visualization will stretch you to deliver on your objectives, and it will potentially take you further than you ever imagined – it affords you wings to fly without limits. However, visualization can be a double-edged sword.

While it can have an amazingly positive impact, it can have a negative impact if it amplifies negative thoughts.

Tor Wager, director of the Cognitive and Affective Neuroscience laboratory at the University of Colorado, described imagination as a neurological reality that can impact our brains and bodies in ways that matter for our wellbeing. Your imagination can be so powerful that it creates connections between your subconscious and your reality. The popular idea of *facing your fears* describes the principle behind exposure therapy, a visualization-based treatment for anxiety and phobias that was developed from advances in our understanding of how mental imagery works. Have you ever been afraid of a barking dog? When we repeatedly hear the same dog barking for a long time, our fear and anxiety begin to dwindle until we feel less afraid. That is exposure therapy in the wild. Researchers have found that we can harness the power of repeated exposure by simply imagining the thing that makes us afraid. By repeatedly visualizing our fears *and* facing them, we can reduce their power.

Visualization is a powerful tool. Merely thinking about moving your muscles and your limbs produces almost the same impact on your biological systems as physically moving your body! This incredible discovery shows how we can bridge the distance between our subconscious and reality through the power of mental imagery driven by imagination.

'Anything you can imagine is real.'

— Pablo Picasso.

Who uses visualization?

Jim Carrey spoke with Oprah in 1997 about how he used visualization to unlock opportunities and pathways toward a successful career. Before his unique style of comedy was embraced by Hollywood, Carrey would drive down the road visualizing how directors and people he respected would start getting interested in him and his work. He visualized things he wanted, telling himself that he already had them and was just on the verge of getting a hold of them.

Further visualizing his success, in 1990 Carrey wrote himself a check for ten million dollars for 'acting services rendered' and post-dated it by five years so that it could be cashed on Thanksgiving in 1995. In 1994, Carrey realized he would make ten million dollars from *Dumb and Dumber.* But that was just the beginning. In 1995, he made fifteen million dollars from *Ace Ventura, When Nature Calls,* and between 1996 and 2000 he went on to make twenty million dollars on each of his next four projects, *The Cable Guy, Liar Liar, Me, Myself and Irene,* and *How the Grinch stole Christmas.*

Arnold Schwarzenegger started visualizing in his teens, seeing himself as Mr. Universe. At age 20, he would seize the trophy in London and become the youngest title-holder in history. When he arrived in California, he visualized himself as a famous movie actor, even with his strong Austrian accent: 'I began visualizing that on August 1, I will be on the set shooting *Terminator* and doing all the physical things it requires. Sure enough, on August 1, I am there in Budapest on the set of *Terminator* 6.' Schwarzenegger applied the same principles later in his career when he visualized himself running the state of California and, sure enough, it happened.

Oprah Winfrey dragged herself out of poverty to become one of the wealthiest women on the planet. She focused early on using visualization. As a child watching her grand-mother work hard, Winfrey said to herself, 'My life won't be like this. My life won't be like this, it will be better.'

Oprah visualized getting a role in *The Color Purple* with a special invitation from Steven Spielberg. Her role in that film became a turning point in her career, earning her an Academy Award nomination. Oprah frequently showcases success stories about positive thinking and discusses the concept of *vision boards*. Her words of wisdom to fans are to 'create the highest, grandest vision possible for your life, because you become what you believe.'

The list of noted people who have used visualization is long, even including rap artists. **Drake** was an unsigned budding rapper when he googled 'craziest residential swimming pools' and saved a lush image as a screensaver on his desktop computer. Seeing this luxurious image daily, he was inspired to work harder until he became a successful rap artist. He saw that image every day, and when he achieved success, he bought the mansion.

So far, we have talked about visualization, but this is just one method under the bigger umbrella of mental imagery. Mental imagery goes beyond our audio-visual senses to integrate all five senses and immerse us in synchronous experiences. The concept of Virtual Reality (VR) offers an excellent explanation of how mental imagery works: the immersion, sensation, and perception intersection.

The principle of virtual reality

In 1968, an American computer scientist named Ivan Sutherland and his student, Bob Sproull, created the first VR headset and named it *The Sword of Damocles*. Decades later, *The Sword of Damocles* has become a mainstream element in the operating systems of gaming sets produced by big tech companies, Facebook, Microsoft, Apple, Amazon, and Google and numerous other companies, cinema offerings, and game centers around the globe.

So, what is virtual reality?

Virtual reality can feel like being teleported to another visual realm with near-perfect mimicry of reality. But why is it that just putting on VR headgear ushers you into another world that feels so real and yet is not? It stems from the fact that our sensory organs work in the same way whether we're in the real world or a visual world created by humans. Our eyes, ears, and nose work the same way whether you are in the real world or VR.

This happens because VR mimics reality. Our brains produce the same response, regardless of whether the experiences that stimulate perceptions are real or virtual. The near-perfect mimicry of reality in VR operates via the interplay of three critical features: *immersion, sensation, and perception.*

Immersion describes how closely a VR environment approximates reality and can be used to gauge the level at which key VR parameters are in sync with the real world. For example, if you can talk in different tones and at various pitch levels in the real world, but can only talk in a restricted number of tones and pitches in VR, then the VR experience of immersion is limited.

Sensation is the ease with which our sensory gates can usher in information from the external environment and process it. Sensation is the effective conveyance of information to the brain via our five senses.

Perception is the process of translating incoming sensory data into information that can be processed by the brain. This is how the brain interprets information from the outside world so that we can understand and navigate through our environment. In VR, the environment is virtual, but our perceptions and responses are as though we are in the real world. A person in VR might walk or feel water gushing from a tap onto their skin. The way the brain interprets the sensations of walking and gushing water is perception.

The interplay between the three elements of immersion, sensation, and perception in the right proportions generates the semblance of reality in VR and is the essence of VR.

Mental imagery is your internal VR ecosystem. Mental imagery is the power of your imagination to create an internal VR that comes across as even more potent than the digital VR (which we traditionally accord the VR title) in every way.

Former American football quarterback Troy Aikman said, 'I always play every game in my mind before it begins. A lot of times in a game a play will happen and it will feel like *deja vu*, like I've seen the play happen before in my mind.'

How to activate mental imagery

For mental imagery to work to your advantage you need to deploy the following steps:

- Clarity: be crystal clear about what you want to achieve from visualization.
- Hold yourself in high esteem and maintain a positive mindset. You need to be confident that the process will deliver as expected and that you are on the right track with the right mindset.
- Bring your mind into the present. Empty your mind and let go of every thought until you're thinking of nothing. This is when you will be ready to start visualizing.
- Focus on the journey, not the outcome, and celebrate small wins. Channel your energies and

attention to the process of pursuing success and not just an outcome. In this way, you will be well-positioned to celebrate the small wins as they come.

- Strike the right balance between clarity and flexibility. While it's great to be crystal clear about how you will achieve your goals, it's also critical to build flexibility into the process and respond to contingencies.

- Be creative by leveraging visuals and images. Your visualization needs to be a complete replica of reality. Once you have drowned out other thoughts and are fully tuned in to the essence of the visualization, you need to imagine everything in your VR from the characters to the features of your environment, to the sounds, all as it would be in reality.

- Work hard at it. Visualization is no different from other skills that you acquire and nurture by investing time, effort, and practice. You must continually practice visualization to become better and better at it with each passing day.

What did we learn?

We saw that mental imagery includes more than just visualization; it incorporates inputs from all five senses, not only audio-visual experiences.

We understood that our cognitive systems process mental imagery in the same way that we process experiences in reality, and this is the principle behind VR.

We saw examples of how people have activated mental imagery and put this to work to transform their lives.

Finally, we learned how to put mental imagery into practice in simple actionable steps.

What's next?

Use the points below to guide you to stimulate the power of your imagination and activate mental imagery:

- Deploy all five senses. Mental imagery includes more than just the visual senses.
- Practice to perfection. Like any other endeavor, mental imagery can be practiced. Devote time to practice to reach perfection.

- Stay true to yourself all the way. This is critical to preserve the originality and integrity of your mental imagery.
- Place yourself at the focal point of your mental imagery. You are the Rock Star! You're the pro-tagonist, the lead actor, so behave like one!

On the next page, you'll find an exercise that will guide you step by step to prepare your vision board. To make it even easier, I have included a sample vision board. Once you have created your vision board, place it at that spot where you simply cannot miss it! That spot where you look several times each day.

Now, let's explore both sides of the power of leverage: leveraging in and leveraging out.

Exercise: Creating a Vision Board

Creating your Vision Board (V-Board)

Step by Step Approach to building your V-Board

Stir up your Creative Brain cells
•Use the most representative image that stirs up the right message you want to stick to your senses

Command Action in a familiar way!
•Write using handwritten sticky notes (in marker) to show the action you require to achieve the image. Use a simple clear phrase to capture the message (Less is more)

Build in a Sense of urgency
•Post in red (using a marker) the timeline to drive this action to fulfilment

Integrate as a Habit
•Place your Visual Board in the area where you pause to reflect the most or where you visit and spend the most time. This could be in your home office, the fridge, beside a big mirror, etc.

Establish Drumbeats
•You must ensure you appraise your progress daily, weekly, monthly. You need to establish dedicated time slots blocked on your calendar when you will do this

Materials Required
- Cardboard / Thick Paper
- Printed Images
- Sticky Notes
- Markers in Colors
- Pins / Glue

A V-Board Sample (my personal example)

MY VISION BOARD EXAMPLE

CHAPTER 5

The Power of Leverage: Leverage In | Leveraging Out

Building internal and external connections

*'Give me a lever long enough and
a fulcrum on which to place it and
I shall move the world.'*

— Archimedes

A t some point in our lives, we have all wondered why people who seemed to put less effort into a project or activity than we did somehow got better results. This might have appeared unfair, but now we know better: some people learn the principle of leverage earlier than others.

We apply the principle of leverage when we use tools to amplify our efforts in daily life. From simple machines at home to complex machines in manufacturing plants, to abstract tools such as the 80-20 Pareto rule, we see leverage. However, that's just the half of it – that is only external leverage. To build robust leverage, we need to combine external leverage with internal leverage.

In this section, you will observe the power of leverage from both sides: leveraging in and leveraging out. You will see how leveraging in is established by mental imagery and reinforced by building the right connections based on the law of attraction, while leveraging out is achieved by scaling up our resources and capabilities to augment our performance levels.

Leveraging in

Let's flashback a bit to a time when you saw a connection between two or more events. It might have been a connection you couldn't quite explain, as the probability of these events being associated with each other seemed inestimably low.

We are going to step into the world of establishing internal connections by synchronicity. Associating events through synchronicity, or occurrence at the same time, is a common phenomenon that we have all experienced, but we will see what drives this association and how we can turn it to our advantage.

I once went into a gym in a country where I had relocated for work; there I experienced something more than just a coincidence. As I got on the treadmill, I saw a friend getting on another treadmill. But that's just the half of it. I had lived on the same street as my friend in a different country before we had gone our separate ways to different countries. And now we found that we had relocated a second time to the same country and were living on the same street, doing the same kind of job, and in very similar apartments. We had not even talked during the years since we had parted ways.. but for some strange reasons, I had thought about him multiple times that month… and now I was seeing him face to face! Every time I think about these layers of coincidence and probability, I am simply amazed. However, on closer examination, we can see that synchronicity is more than layers of coincidence.

Synchronicity can be thought of as the alignment of your wishes and desires with events that are completely in line with those desires. This simultaneous occurrence is statistically improbable but happens nonetheless, connecting your intentionality and activity in one go.

A child might have a huge desire for ice cream and suddenly his aunt comes to visit, bringing two vanilla ice cream cups without having called or aligned with the child or her mother.

Bringing it home, let me tell you about a very recent experience. A few days into starting this chapter on leveraging in and out, I got so deeply immersed in my writing on a Saturday morning that I worked non-stop from around 7 a.m. until 2 p.m. I then decided to take a break, have my first meal of the day, and relax before getting back into it later that evening. As I walked up the stairs, my phone beeped and I got a message from a friend of mine to review an article he wrote about the power of leverage. I was amazed and then I smiled to myself – synchronicity!

Synchronicity

The concept of *synchronizität*, German for synchronicity, was first introduced by analytical psychologist Carl Jung. It holds that events are *meaningful coincidences* if they occur with no causal relationship yet seem to be meaningfully related. The Greek roots of *synchronicity* are *syn*, meaning together, and *khronos*, meaning time. *Synchronicity* is 'occurring together in time.'

We often talk about ideas that are in sync or music beats that are synchronized. These co-occurring events seem to be characterized by the elements of luck, chance, or coincidence.

In *Entangled Minds*, Dean Radin explained that the psychic phenomena many people believe to be behind synchronous events are real and widespread. Scientific findings indicate that synchronicity is an inevitable consequence of the interconnected and entangled physical reality we live in, as described by Albert Einstein's quantum physics: we experience coincidental events that seem 'spooky at a distance' but that exist as quantum entanglements.

Quantum entanglements are the ways two discrete objects stay connected through time and space, long after their initial interaction and without any conventional communication. The question is, is it possible that a similar entanglement of minds would explain the mystery of apparently psychic abilities? Dean Radin showed that psychic phenomena such as telepathy, clairvoyance, and psychokinesis, are real occurrences.

In our example of the child who wanted ice cream, the child released some force fields through their thoughts that caught up with similar thoughts emitted from his aunt and found a way to co-exist, creating the interconnection required for synchronicity.

Dr. Phil Merry did a Ph.D. program on synchronicity and explains this phenomenon as 'a meaningful coincidence' that provides guidance or direction to individuals or groups. According to Merry, specific steps must be undertaken to create a pathway for synchronicity in our lives.

- First, have a strong feeling about something you believe in and back that up with a strong desire that drives you, like your purpose in the form of your passion, principles, or skills.
- Next, trust your intuition. This sounds easier than it is, as our decisions may be influenced by rational thinking. Normally, this rational thinking would need to be balanced with intuition.
- Third, be on the lookout for strange coincidences that may not seem logically linked – they are the perfect drivers of synchronicity.
- Fourth, make a point to reflect and connect the dots to truly observe the power of synchronicity in the current context, and focus on how you can leverage it to your advantage.

- Finally, for synchronicity to be fully entrenched, we must stay in the present and bring our sensibilities into our current state of mind.

When we follow these steps, we will cultivate the habit of allowing synchronicity to thrive in our lives and leverage its impact by steering it in the right course. By doing this, we will observe that we're not alone; we're connected through magnetic fields of energy that we can use to guide our footsteps, our actions, and our thoughts to maximize our activities.

You have the power to attract that
which you desire through clear intent
and strong emotion.

Research in quantum physics, biology, and psychology shows that we can connect with fields of energy that are 'answers from the universe.' To leverage synchronicity, we must investigate the signs that call on us.

Synchronization is a powerful phenomenon that exists across the globe. However, we often fail to consider synchronicity, as it's commonly classified as coincidental occurrences or fortuitous activities – what people tag as luck.

But how do we tap into it?

First things first

To benefit from the power of synchronicity, we need first to recognize that these elements exist.

In the last couple of decades, quantum theory has proven that synchronous events exist. According to quantum physics, humans are 99.9% energy and just 0.1% matter. We're balls of moving energy. And, as with energy, we have multiplicities of connection and attraction with each other.

Secondly

We need to be crystal clear about how to leverage synchronicity. When you know you have a potential power of some sort or a specific skill, the way you convey yourself is entirely different than if you believe the effects of your activity relied on pure luck. This is because your perceptions affect your interactions with others. Similarly, knowing you have achieved something original gives you the confidence and boldness to deploy your achievement. With the knowledge that you are part of quantum entanglements, you can seek to leverage it.

First, you need to understand or recognize synchronicity, next you need to understand it exists and is available on a widespread basis – available to all, including you, and you can leverage it just as others can.

Finally

You need to activate the innate power of synchronicity by deliberately infusing it into your plans and building networks and connections that will allow you to maximize synchronicity and act on it.

Remember, it's one thing to admit that synchronicity exists, but it's another to build synchronicity into your overall activity, and then it's an entirely different thing to execute your plans in line with this understanding.

Leveraging out

Leveraging out, or externally, is based on the common understanding of leverage. Leveraging out is a technique used to multiply or disproportionately increase output based on specific inputs. This powerful concept can amplify your inputs and allow you to achieve more of your goals across various endeavors. Leveraging can magnify your inputs to deliver 1+1=3, amplifying your inputs to generate disproportionate outputs.

*'I would rather earn 1% off
a hundred people's efforts than
100% off my own efforts.'*

— J. Paul Getty, American Industrialist

This concept cuts across all endeavors, from education to career-building, business, marketing, finance, home-building, and more; and it helps you to re-invest in your knowledge base by learning from the *mistakes* or *experiences of others* who have already made those mistakes or passed through similar terrain.

When we understand the basic principles of leveraging out, we can re-apply them easily and practically in our day-to-day endeavors. We need to think of leveraging out as the most efficient way to multiply our efforts to deliver the maximum possible output.

Examples of leveraging out

Let's now see this concept in some real-world applications before consolidating what we have learned and considering some key areas where we can deploy leveraging out.

Tree planting

Leveraging out can be understood as a *divide-to-multiply* concept. Let's think about divide-to-multiply in terms of day-to-day life. Take the example of increasing the number of trees in a forest. First, you might 'cut a part' of the tree by getting seeds to plant. By doing this, you end up with more trees. We find strong parallels to this in business franchising when a company divides itself by partnering strategically with local experts to gain entry into new markets and 'multiply' itself again.

Hunting strategies

Another way to see leveraging out is to compare the hunting skills of the king of the jungle with those of the spider. *Would you rather hunt like a lion or a spider?* A lion hunts when hungry and either stalks his prey or hunts with others. Either way, lions hunt opportunistically, as needed. On the other hand, the spider hunts strategically. It translates its efforts into building a web where it can sit back and watch as its prey comes to it. Spiders adopt the power of leverage.

'The richest people in the world
look for and build networks,
everyone else looks for work.'

— Robert Kiyosaki

Leveraging out with systems

Systems establish a framework that incorporates as many input resources as possible. With systems, you will have a scalable platform that can take you to unimaginable levels. The McDonalds business model is a great illustration of adopting systems by piggy-backing on OPM/OPT (other people's money and other people's time) and franchising to create leverage.

Levering out financially

Financial leverage is the use of debt in the form of bor-rowed money to finance the purchase of assets. It gen-erates positive returns when the borrowed money is used to generate more money than the interest incurred by the debt. Companies balance acquiring debt for leverage with equity. This may reduce the EPS (earn-ings per share) of the company shareholders, but as long as the leverage (borrowed capital) can potentially accelerate returns, the investment will typically pay out.

Leveraging out your achievements

Being able to achieve your goals is awesome. But what's even more awesome is scaling up that achievement to pave the way for even more achievements, just by positioning yourself as a brand. Your previous achievements can act as a springboard to marketing yourself as a brand, opening up even more avenues.

The most decked-up Olympian, swimmer Michael Phelps, leveraged his swimming achievements to unlock massive endorsement deals worth ten million dollars annually from sponsors like Speedo, Ping, and Wheaties. Looking inwards, ask yourself, 'How can I leverage a recent achievement, award, or recognition to generate a new deal, better compensation, or open up new avenues for business?'

Leveraging out your relationships via connections

We're all human before we're CEOs, authors, business managers, doctors, leaders, supervisors, or other professionals. This means our decisions will always be subjective and skewed, so we need to feel comfortable with the people we work with to bolster our trust, reduce barriers to efficiency and productivity, and open up opportunities to scale our business to our mutual advantage. How can we build trust? Relationships are critical and building strong connections can fast-track your engagement with decision-makers at target companies, facilitate your shortlisting into an entrepreneur incubator circle, or even alert you to a potential position ahead of the crowd. Connections are a valuable component of leverage in business, as you can scale up your knowledge base and skill-set through the flow of information within your circle. The list of gains that can be amassed by leveraging your connections is endless.

Leveraging out in businesses

According to John Nieuwenburg, there are seven forms of leverage in business:

1. OPM (Other People's Money): debt, the stock market.
2. OPT (Other People's Time): employees, hiring freelancers.

3. OPW (Other People's Work): franchising your business.
4. OPE (Other People's Experiences): get a mentor or a coach. Read books, blogs, etc.
5. OPI (Other People's Ideas): venture capitalists use other people's ideas to make their own money grow.
6. Scalable Production & Distribution: Amazon, Costco, and Walmart.
7. Scalable Customer Base: iTunes, Evernote, Dropbox.

Company boards can further translate their mission, vision, and strategy downstream to all employees within the organization. This can be done by tapping into their workforce's intrinsic and extrinsic motivation, capability systems, feedback, and access to company ownership, via company shares and other means, to ensure employees co-own their vision.

Leveraging out doing more with less: Vilfredo Pareto

Leverage can be achieved by adopting the Pareto principle, which can also be called the *principle of imbalance*.

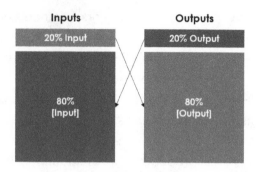

ILLUSTRATION OF PARETO'S 80/20 PRINCIPLE OF IMBALANCE

Here are a few imbalances that you have probably seen at some point in your life:

- 80% of outputs are generated by 20% of inputs.
- 80% of results come from 20% of the effort.
- 80% of the world's riches are concentrated in 20% of developed countries.
- 80% of sales or profit comes from 20% of customers, products, or services.
- 80% of the time we wear 20% of our clothes.
- 80% of a warehouse's stock comes from 20% of suppliers.
- 80% of criminal activities are performed by 20% of the population.
- 80% of the time you visit only 20% of your friends or relatives.
- 80% of readers will read only 20% of this book!

In these examples, there is an amazing 16:1 ratio of performance between the two groups. So, the average income of people in the top 20% is 16 times greater than the average income of those in the bottom 80%.

Taking this line of thinking further, what if you could extract the top 20% of the top 20%... how would this translate to outputs?

- The top 20% of the top 20% (the top 4%) would deliver an output of 80% of 80% (64%). So, we could say the top 4% would generate 64% of output.
- The next top 20% of the top 20% of the top 20% (top 0.8%) would turn around an output of 80% x 80% x 80% (51.2%). So, the top 0.8% would generate 51.2% of total output. In simple terms, the top 1% would generate more than half of all output.

Similarly, we can understand the rate of redundancy when we move outwards from the top 20%. Considering categories across products, brands, or SKUs (standard keeping units), value (sales revenue and profit), and the cumulative percentage of the values, all sorted in decreasing order of value, it's not uncommon for analysis to show that the top 20% of products contributes 80% of the profit, the next 40% generates 20% of the profit, and the bottom 40% makes no contribution to profitability yet uses up inventory, dollars, and warehouse space.

ADAPTED FROM: SIMAFORE LLC & STRAT-WISE LLC (2012). HOW TO IMPLEMENT THE 80-20 PRINCIPLE IN BUSINESS

Applying the 80-20 Rule

Besides pointing out the obvious imbalance in every facet of life, the 80-20 principle also reveals major opportunities for improvements:

- **In sales**, if we redirect focus from the trivial 80% to more of the vital 20%, we can increase value per input or resource.
- **In business management**, we can contract out management of the trivial 80% to specialists and

use less time and fewer resources on it while gradually growing its value.

- **In relationships**, we can refocus our time and energy on the top 20% to achieve more happiness, contentment, and development. We need to ensure we nurture these relationships to create more value for ourselves.
- **In our health**, we can seek to consume more of those foods that provide nutritional benefits and scale down on the foods that don't refresh us.

Establishing the connections

As I stated in Chapter 2, establishing the right connections hinges on the idea that the sum of the whole is greater than the constituent parts. Remember that popular African proverb: 'If you want to go fast, go alone, but if you want to go far, go together.' We can't achieve our overall vision by walking alone. We need to build scale, integrate resources, and complement our gaps to leverage opportunities that strengthen our chances of winning.

When we put these elements in place, we activate the law of attraction via the vehicle of synchronicity. Nature itself embraces synchronicity. Trees can sync with each other in movement and growth, fish move together in synchronized schools, and birds erupt into a dawn chorus as if pre-planned and well-orchestrated. The list is long, and even inanimate objects become synchronized within natural systems and forces such as gravity, wave motion, and global weather patterns. Overall, we see a strong tendency to order in animate and inanimate nature; through the laws of attraction, we establish many fortuitous connections that work to progress our goals.

To ensure we get the desired output from leveraging in and out, we need to execute *both* and not *either*. We need to create the right leverage internally by setting our mental imagery in place to take advantage of synchronicities. This will ensure we're fully prepared to max out opportunities as they arise. Simultaneously, we need to leverage out by maximizing our inputs through scaled efforts and delivering disproportionate outputs, by focusing more strongly on the vital few and redirecting core resources away from the trivial majority.

The art of establishing the right connections between leveraging in and leveraging out will activate the exponential impacts we achieve for every input, leading to unparalleled efficiencies.

The power of alignment

Leveraging out thrives on the adage that 'opportunity meets preparedness.' This concept underlies the idea of turning around a synchronous activity that we would usually do for fun, into a tool that works for us. Alignment as a leveraging-out tool involves matching a benchmark standard to improve your performance above the standard. This is a form of 'resonance.' To explain this further, let's take a quick dash into the world of athletics and one of the greatest athletes of all time, who still holds amazing records on the racetrack, Usain Bolt. Let's talk a bit about the strategy deployed by Bolt in achieving breakthrough results in the world of athletics.

Usain Bolt

Across the globe, Usain Bolt is probably the name most synonymous with speed. It's easy to understand why, as no one has matched his achievements on the race track. Bolt is considered the greatest sprinter of all time. The eight-time Olympic gold medalist, whose nickname is 'Lightning Bolt', was the first man in history to set three world records in a single Olympic Games competition, which he did in Beijing in 2008. He made history by breaking his own records and completing the 100-meter race in just 9.69 seconds.

BOLT DOMINATING THE PACK AT THE 2016 RIO OLYMPICS

Outside the Olympics, Bolt is an eleven-time world champ. Bolt also showed that he understands the principle of mental imagery when he said that 'learning the mind is as important as understanding the body.'

So, the question is, how did Bolt achieve all of this? What was his strategy, what did he do behind the scenes? The legend we know as Lightning Bolt had a couple of things working against his success – his height and his build.

Bolt's height – a disadvantage?

Standing at 6'5 (1.96 meters), Bolt is one of the tallest athletes in the history of sprinting. Most physiologists would predict that Bolt's height would put him at a disadvantage, as a height of just under six feet is considered essential for running a sub-ten second 100-meters. 'Bigger people are going be slower out of the blocks,' wrote Andrew Udofa, a doctoral researcher at Southern Methodist University. A similar conclusion was shared by a paper published in the *Journal of Sports and Medicine* that showed big guys have physics working against them. Acceleration is proportional to the force produced, but inversely proportional to body mass, according to Newton's second law. This means there is an inverse relationship between height and performance in sports such as sprinting, especially when you cross a height threshold identified as being around 6-feet tall. Simply put, it would be a Herculean task to produce enough power to overcome the drag of a big body. Bolt himself insisted that his height was a disadvantage at the start of a race, but that it gave him the edge on his competitors once he got going because he has more force than they once he gets out of the blocks.

Bolt's struggle with scoliosis

Scoliosis is a sideways curvature of the spine that occurs mostly during the growth spurt just before puberty. Scoliosis was a major deterrent to Bolt in his running career, especially early on, and was responsible for numerous injuries. Bolt's scoliosis was the bane of his running career and led to asymmetrical legs and uneven strides. But Bolt leveraged these disadvantages outwards through alignment in the form of resonance.

Bolt's strategy: Aligning to win

Research by Professor Michael J. Richardson of Cincinnati University uncovered an interesting discovery; it showed that the Jamaican superstar sprinter leveraged a critical asset to outperform his opponents: the capability to sync his race with his opponent's race. Professor Richardson studied every frame from the Berlin 2009 World Championship final when Usain Bolt set a new world record. According to Richardson, about 30% of Bolt's steps were in sync with the next best and his major competition, Tyson Gay.

According to Jonah Lehrer, what makes this synchronization so surprising is that due to his height, Bolt has an extremely long stride. It took him only 41 steps to cross the finish line, four or five steps fewer than Gay, who took 45–46 steps. Despite the significant differences in body type and overall physique between the sprinters, Bolt ensured they stayed in sync up to 30% of the time and in resonance with each other.

Researchers Varlet and Richardson demonstrated that Bolt and Gay, who ran side by side throughout the race in Berlin, spontaneously and intermittently synchronized their steps. Even optimized individual motor skills can be modulated by the simple presence of another individual, via interpersonal coordination processes that are driven by external rhythms. We see some of the phenomenon of benefitting from external rhythms when we listen to pop music while exercising. What these examples tell us is that alignment is great for performance, but it needs to match the right benchmarks to be optimal.

When opportunity meets preparedness

Let's go back in time to 2007 in the U.S., when two friends who were graduates of the Rhode Island School of Design had just moved from New York to San Francisco to establish their careers. These young dudes, Brian Chesky and Joe Gebbia were both 25 at the time. They were struggling to pay their rent with the rising cost of housing and were looking for ways to make some extra cash. They identified an opportunity when they observed that hotel rooms around the city were fully booked during a certain local industrial design conference. They decided to explore hiring out their living space to willing customers during the conference in return for cash. They quickly built a website, acquired some mattresses, and had sold out their spaces in no time. This, of course, was the birth of one of the most fascinating disruptive business models in history, Airbnb, as we know it today.

The critical point is that opportunities cut across every dimension you can imagine. It's up to us to be ready to leverage these opportunities to the fullest.

What opportunity are you set to leverage right now?

What did we learn?

We have observed the power of leverage from two critical viewpoints: internal and external. We saw how synchronicity can activate our internal leverage, building up mental imagery and facilitating the right connections based on the law of attraction.

We explored leveraging outwards by deploying tools and techniques to do more with less. We saw how to establish the right connections by building scale, integrating resources, and complementing gaps.

With leveraging in and out clearly in place, there is an obvious need for a lifestyle shift as we move to the execution stage.

What's next?

Through the power of leverage, our productivity levels can skyrocket, but we still need to build on a solid framework to ensure we implement it effectively. How?

- By establishing the right foundation through mental imagery.

- By building off your leverage by first *leveraging in*, based on your established mental imagery process.
- By connecting through *leveraging out.*
- By practicing to perfection. Repeat the steps above, but ensure each step remains interconnected to form a feedback loop.

On the next page, you will see a visual representation of this framework, which may serve as a catalyst to 'disrupting your methods.' With the power of leverage fully understood, you will learn in the next chapter how to develop a positive lifestyle shift as you continue to gain momentum.

2] Disrupt your Methods- *Create New Powerful Connections*

Understanding Mental Imagery
The Power to Create from within

Leveraging In
Building the right connections via the law of attraction

Leveraging Out
Building synergies with tools, techniques and resources on the right knowledge base

ADAPTED FROM *"3 STEPS TO ACHIEVING YOUR GOALS"*. SOURCE: *IMOWO ENANG*

93

CHAPTER 6

Lifestyle Shift

Operating at your peak

What is more critical to you? Pacing yourself to spread your energy over the day, or expending considerable energy per activity?

Some people can maintain peak levels of performance in only short bursts, others find a way to maintain fair levels of performance over time, but a select few can sustain peak performance all the time.

In this chapter, you will look at critical themes for achieving the peak performance you have always wanted... and how to maintain it over time. You will see that while time management is key to driving productivity, energy management ensures you're equipped to sustain productivity levels. You will observe the key elements of productivity being unpacked. To drive sustained performance, you will also explore how other critical inputs, such as food, impact productivity and focus levels, and how our maintenance cycle – our sleep time – remains a key contributor to nourishing our mental capabilities.

Accelerate your energy levels

Many people were caught up in the time management fad in which improvement in time management was thought to accelerate productivity to amazing levels. While time management is important, it is just a part of the whole solution. No matter how skilled you are and how efficiently you have planned your time, if you're low on energy you're on your way to logging out or even shutting down on that task.

> *'The difference between one man and another is not mere ability, it's energy.'*

> — Thomas Arnold

Energy management is a key factor for delivering an efficient output; it is triggered and sustained by passion. As Warren Buffet said, 'Without passion, you don't have energy. Without energy, you have nothing.'

Though we each have the same 24 hours in a day, our outputs are as different as our fingerprints. It's all a matter of how we manage our productivity, and that is a byproduct of our energy management.

I have seen my output grow exponentially by adopting this principle. I used to think I could activate productivity with a long list of projects with timelines and that I needed to rigorously track my activity. While this looked good on paper, I would repeatedly burn out and need to spend time to recover – and even more time to get back to my earlier levels of productivity. I recall vividly how I would try to evaluate my net output *vis a vis* my input and just not be able to place a finger on growth.

I had also believed that all I needed to do to improve my performance was plug in more hours. So, I traded sleep for productivity, or so I thought! I learned that there is indeed a tipping point at which any hour traded for sleep leads to critical productivity losses. Once you cross that threshold, every minute of sleep lost to work will yield many more minutes of lost productivity and burnout. To avoid this vicious cycle of declining pro-ductivity, I needed to manage my energy as well as my time.

Manage your energy and your time

Have you ever asked yourself why, even with our work-rooms teeming with efficiency tools, we sometimes find a gap in productivity? Smartphones and e-calen-dars might enhance our time management, but is that enough? We need to establish the right energy man-agement framework to achieve productivity goals.

The issue is, how can one maintain energy at peak levels to complete expected tasks within a specific time frame? We will be exploring some simple steps to ensure we can maintain effective energy levels.

Identify your energy cycle

Some people say, 'I am a morning person and I need to start early when the sun rises so I can feel my inner strength rise with the sun!' Others say, 'I'm a night person and I love working late, as I get better as the day draws to a close.' I went to boarding school, with six years of rules and regulations and rigid schedules. That was where I learned that I loved to get up early to stay ahead of schedule. As I grew older, this trait grew with me. By the time I went to college, you could count on seeing me first in class, and it was the same for my second degree. When I started work, I would be the first in the office and one of the first to leave. This was my way of life – get in early and get out early.

Later, when I changed roles and locations, I saw that one of my senior executives started late and worked late into the evening, churning out work with high productivity. I decided to emulate him, as he came across as a superstar. But when I tried the late-start, late-finish approach I failed woefully. My efficiency didn't increase as the day went on. If anything, my efficiency was significantly lower; I felt that I had a poor start to the day and then struggled to play catch up, rather than leading with a head start. The thing is, there's no one-size-fits-all approach, as we're all wired differently.

Ride on your energy bursts

It's important to identify the times when you have been at your energy peak. Once you're able to identify this peak, you can build a schedule that leverages your most efficient and effective work styles. So, how can you achieve this?

Ask yourself a few questions:

- What preceded the activities: how did you start the day?
- What were the activities and how did you execute them? Did you use a specific method? Did you leverage some existing work? How did you deliver on this activity?
- What was your motivation to do this activity so efficiently?

Once you have answered these questions, you can work out what, how, and why you can generate sustainable bursts of energy, and this will equip you as you build a schedule that will allow you to ride on your energy levels based on need and circumstance.

Reinventing your work schedule

Reorganize your schedule based on your most productive times by blocking out your high-priority tasks against the periods when your energy is at its highest. This is especially critical for tasks requiring more mental focus and discipline. If you're an early riser, try to schedule your most important activities as early in the day as possible and push the less important tasks further into the day. If you're more of a night owl, try to move critical tasks to the times when you reach high energy levels to deliver excellence in your execution.

Nothing is cast in stone, and the right mix will be up to you. The most critical thing is diagnosing your energy levels over the day to understand how to ride on your bursts of energy and schedule an activity system that builds on this.

Let's explore how we can increase our output by first accelerating our work levels or productivity.

Accelerating work levels

Productivity is a function of how much output we produce within a timeframe. We can understand this as a ratio that describes the rate at which we can generate output:

$$\text{Productivity} = \frac{\text{Output}}{\text{Time}}$$

Our productivity is simply the rate at which we turn around output for a particular activity. We can accelerate productivity in three ways:

1. Increase our output per time.
2. Decrease our time per output.
3. A combination of both.

Increasing your output

According to Andrew Grove, output can be defined as our activity further accelerated by leverage. We can revise our formula for productivity accordingly:

$$\text{Productivity} = \frac{\text{Output}}{\text{Time}} = \frac{\text{Leverage X Activity}}{\text{Time}}$$

Leverage helps to multiply output and generate higher returns with the same input. Some of the ways we can do this are by using the 4 'REs': *re*qualifying, *re*grouping, *re*scheduling, and *re*diverting.

Requalifying

To ensure we fully optimize our workflow, we may need to requalify our activity system. To do this, we can assess each element and process flow to monitor whether we're executing only the activities that bring value from our different stakeholders' perspectives. We need to learn to step back and reassess the cycle, as in a 'value stream mapping' exercise in lean theory. This reassessment will expose value-adding tasks that need increased focus and non-value-adding tasks that we need to cut down to a reasonable level to eliminate 'waste.' Reassessing our system can lead to a requalified process that delivers greater value while redirecting resources to more efficient outputs for less cost and use of resources overall.

To illustrate, let's say you have been preparing business updates to go out within the quarter to inform stakeholders about progress while asking for action-based responses. In the requalifying process, you would first assess the steps you usually take:

- Is the information user-friendly? Does it include the information needed?
- How can more be said with less?
- Are there details that can be communicated on other platforms?
- Can you automate the process further: data gathering and sharing, templates, communication cycles?

Once you have answered these questions and identified relevant actions to take, you will have moved in the right direction to requalify your activity system.

Regrouping

Some activities are best handled in bundles, as they share similar attributes and can be quickly scaled up to continually accelerate productivity. Regrouping does help. For example, you may group sessions of focus groups with key employees, and sessions of feedback or coaching with others in the same activity. If you can connect with these groups within the same timeframe and while wearing the same hat, you create more efficiency than if you tackled the same tasks in a series.

Rescheduling

It seems commonplace, but many efficiencies can be made just by aligning meetings, activities, or projects at the right time. Leverage the use of automated calendars. I have noticed that I function better with one professional and one personal calendar. Most of the time, we prioritize only our professional tasks. Coordinating your professional activity is great, but we should also prioritize personal time. Keep separate personal and professional calendars.

Rediverting

Some tasks, activities, and services do not need to be handled by you alone. It's critical to continually build your team's capabilities. Building your team's capabilities will help you multiply yourself and free up time to reinvest in more critical activities without dropping the ball on your diverted tasks. Delegation is the watchword.

Everyone will need to delegate at some point. To delegate effectively, we can ask ourselves some questions:

- Do I really need to do this task?
- How important is this task?

As a rule, you will be more inclined to delegate less strategic or critical tasks. Delegation should build capability in team members and motivate them by creating opportunities to undertake more challenging activities. This creates a win-win-win for you, your team member, and the end receivers or stakeholders receiving value from the task.

Key points:

- You will still own the results of the delegated tasks: delegating the task doesn't take you out of the woods when there are issues!
- Check that your expectations and those of team members are in sync.
- Provide the right tools and resources for the activities to be carried out, and allow team members to carry out delegated tasks autonomously and creatively.

Motivation

Nothing matters like motivation. Motivation is the engine that keeps us firing on all cylinders, keeps the energy coming, and keeps hope alive. However, there are times when doing anything other than what you've been scheduled to do is attractive. As an undergraduate student, during preps for exams on my toughest course, anything else on the planet was more interesting to me than studying for that course! Even the most diligent and inspiring people experience motivation droughts and need to refuel.

This cycle of motivation loss and gain is one most of us can relate to. You may have visualized completing a task and generated mental imagery in sync with this goal. You may have been set to deliver a super-productive day as you launched into that activity. But you decided first to bring yourself up to speed on the events of the day instead of making a start on the task, and then one activity led to another. You checked social media and hopped from one platform to another, easily losing an hour or more.

These motivational blocks are due to the difficulty of overcoming the inertia of not starting the task. This only happens when we aren't strongly motivated, as motivation is the ignition that sparks the car. Once that inertia is overcome, maintaining your speed is much easier – because you're now accelerating.

You are what you eat

Reflect on your most productive time either face to face in the office or working from home or a remote workstation. Can you recall what you ate that day? Breakfast, lunch, dinner...in between?

When we think about the inputs of high-level performance at work, the type of food we eat is unlikely to be identified as critical for productivity. We tend to think of food as just the fuel needed to keep us moving. Some may even see food as something we just have to take in to live, so it becomes merely a survival input.

At some points, I thought of food and the need to refuel as a distraction from work. I wished I could just take one pill that would have all the food I needed. I remember watching a cartoon long ago, *The Jetsons,* where George Jetson had a meal packed into a pill! At the time, I thought that would lead to intense productivity, and I would certainly advocate for a meal in a pill.

But coming back to reality, the truth is that the food we eat is much more important than simple fuel for survival. The composition of the food we eat has a direct impact on the productivity levels we can anticipate. That's why the saying goes, 'we are what we eat.'

Research has shown that our mental and physical status is directly linked to the food and drink we consume. The composition of our food determines the composition of our cell membranes, biochemistry, hormones, and tissues. Our cells are constantly taking up components as they replace themselves, using the food we eat as the renewing source of these components. This means that the composition of our food can affect the quality of even our DNA itself.

Being cautious about what we eat is important, but how we consume it is equally important. Any time we eat while in a negative state of mind, such as the mindset driven by a bad experience or an argument, we can trigger digestive activity that is not adaptive. We could experience this as indigestion. Attending to our mental health before we eat will allow our gut to send the right signals to our brain's emotion centers, enabling our digestive system to work on digestion.

Food also has a direct connection or relationship with cognitive performance. A bad lunch can end up distorting our decision-making and lead to a bad day at work.

In humans, the brain accounts for ~2% of the body weight, but it consumes ~20% of our daily energy intake. It is the body's main consumer of glucose, which is derived from the food we eat. This glucose acts as fuel for the mental engine of the brain. If we get low on fuel, we starve our brain of energy and gradually lose focus and become more easily distracted and reactive. This explains why when some people get hungry, they lose focus and find it difficult to concentrate on tasks or deliverables. The foods we consume have a huge impact on brain function and influence everything from learning to our memory function, even our emotions.

So, yes, we need to take in fuel, but we also need to think about the type of fuel we take in. Two dynamics must be considered on this score: first, the time it takes our digestive system to convert the food we have eaten into energy; and, second, the effort or energy needed for our digestive system to convert the food into this energy that can sustain us.

The digestive system takes different amounts of time to convert the different foods we eat into energy, and this corresponds to the different processes by which they are converted. In practice, different foods deliver different returns in energy and they affect our productivity in different ways. When deciding what foods and meals will boost productivity, consider:

- How you can maintain your glucose levels to avoid losing your focus and concentration.
- Foods that are processed quickly and provide energy faster may also lead to a steep energy drop once the energy is used.

- Fast foods may seem convenient until you find you are experiencing drops in your overall performance.
- Fruits and vegetables have been shown to increase engagement, focus, and creativity and can be part of every meal.

Stay active, stay awesome

A survey of 2000 men and women done by Stefano Passa Rello showed that engaging in sports improves our mood, morale, and motivation, leading to a positive impact on productivity at work (observed in 47% of women and 40% of men). The kinds of activities that matter include any sport, exercise, or physical recreation. According to Angela Duckworth's *Grit,* kids who participate in extracurricular activities tend to fare better not just in grades but also in self-esteem. Follow-through in such activities was a critical indicator of success in young people, with a good number of those who excelled later in life having participated in at least two high school extracurricular activities for several years, while making significant advancements, such as holding leadership roles

Elementary studies have shown that exercise helps the brain function well. A basic understanding of biology tells us that when we exercise, more blood flows to the brain, and brain activity increases. Research shows that more exercise means more blood flow, and more blood flow means more energy and oxygen, leading to better brain performance.

The hippocampus, a part of the brain critical for learning and memory, becomes more active during increased physical activity such as exercise or other recreation. Movement revs up our neurons and improves our cognitive capabilities. Indeed, physical activities can reverse the hippocampal shrinkage that occurs with age. Research carried out in 2008 by John J. Ratey, a Harvard University psychiatrist has shown that those who exercise or play sports outperform their less athletic peers academically.

An interesting report by Anthony Carboni of Princeton University shows that exercise helps to organize your brain cells to handle stress better. However, we also know that younger neurons get more excited within the hippocampus when we engage in physical activity. Straight-line thinking would lead us to believe that more exercise should increase our stress levels behind these young, excited neurons, but this isn't the case. Why?

In Carboni's study, two sets of mice were observed: one set of super-active mice and another set of super-lazy mice. The two groups were dunked into a cold swimming pool, and the brains of the two groups responded completely differently. In the lazy mice, researchers found an increase in *immediate-early* genes that are turned on the moment a neuron is fired. The converse happened in the active mice. The *immediate-early* genes were not turned on as they were in the lazy mice, even though the super-active mice had even more excitable neurons. This interesting phenomenon came about due to the release of a neuron transmitter called GABA (Glutamate and gamma-aminobutyric acid) which helps control the excitable neurons of the brain and keep them in check. GABA helps regulate the activity of the brain and tells it when to relax. For the super-active mice, GABA prevented neurons from overreacting to the stress of the cold-water shock and allowed them to manage the stress better.

Carboni further explained that this process helps to explain the fight-or-flight response whereby the brain of a fit, healthy person handles stress better than the brain of a less active person, as it is used to performing at optimum levels under stress. For a less active person, the body goes into overdrive to accommodate sudden stresses and anxiety, and this can lead to burnout. In this way, regular exercise 'vaccinates' the body and brain against daily stressors by facilitating a proactive response.

How to stay active?

Now, we know the importance of staying active and how this affects our productivity levels through the energy levels we're able to sustain. Aside from work, we need to stay active on a personal level to promote cardiovascular health, manage our weight, lower cholesterol levels, and reduce risks of diseases such as diabetes. Staying active also helps us maintain healthy blood pressure and strong bones. The list of benefits goes on, but the question is, what is the right amount of exercise? As with anything else in life, exercising in excess can have deleterious effects. So, how do we strike a balance that will give us health benefits, increased productivity, and higher levels of energy for work?

Major authorities on health recommend that adults need between 75 to 150 minutes of exercise per week. The NHS advises that 'Adults should do some type of physical activity every day. Any type of activity is good for you. The more you do the better.'

Adults should:

- Aim to be physically active every day. Any activity is better than none, and more is better still.
- Do strengthening activities that work all the major muscles (legs, hips, back, abdomen, chest, shoulders, and arms) at least two days a week.

- Do at least 150 minutes of moderate-intensity activity a week or 75 minutes of vigorous-intensity activity a week.
- Reduce the time spent sitting or lying down and break up long periods of inactivity with some activity.

As always, there is no one-size-fits-all approach. I started with less than 75 minutes of moderate exercise per week and when I gained some momentum, I increased my sessions to 150 minutes. I try to do this five days a week for 30 minutes per day, resting for two days. The following scenario outlines three options suggested by the Centers for Disease Control and Prevention.

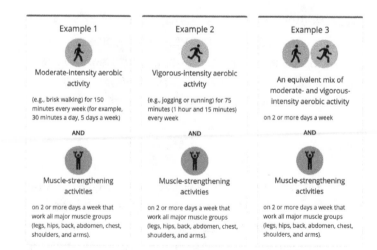

Example 1	Example 2	Example 3
Moderate-intensity aerobic activity	Vigorous-intensity aerobic activity	An equivalent mix of moderate- and vigorous-intensity aerobic activity
(e.g., brisk walking) for 150 minutes every week (for example, 30 minutes a day, 5 days a week)	(e.g., jogging or running) for 75 minutes (1 hour and 15 minutes) every week	on 2 or more days a week
AND	AND	AND
Muscle-strengthening activities	Muscle-strengthening activities	Muscle-strengthening activities
on 2 or more days a week that work all major muscle groups (legs, hips, back, abdomen, chest, shoulders, and arms).	on 2 or more days a week that work all major muscle groups (legs, hips, back, abdomen, chest, shoulders, and arms).	on 2 or more days a week that work all major muscle groups (legs, hips, back, abdomen, chest, shoulders, and arms).

Source: Centers for Disease Control and Prevention

Walk with the brainchild

Our brains are truly a mystery. It's incredible how an organ just about the size of our two fists controls all functions within our bodies – it is by far the most complex structure on the planet. Inside the wonder called the brain, we have the cerebral cortex that comprises almost 80% of our brain mass and enables higher cognition. In the cerebral cortex, our total grey matter is seven times greater than that of other mammals, with a network power city of more than one hundred billion neurons, 100,000 km of interconnections, and an estimated storage capacity of a million gigabytes.

This powerful super-machine never takes a break. Even when we're sleeping, it's not. Therefore, we need to support this engine to ensure it continues to deliver and has sufficient time to replenish.

In previous chapters, we talked about ways we can accelerate our brainpower to become more efficient and productive, personally and professionally. Eating the right foods, exercising, and taking adequate breaks go a long way to enhancing our brainpower. However, there are three critical things the brain needs that we often take for granted:

1. The brain needs sleep

According to a publication from the Sleep Foundation, a OneCare media company, adults aged between 18 and 64 need seven to nine hours of sleep per night. Adults over 65 need seven to eight hours. However, in 2017–18, 32.6% of working adults reported sleeping six or fewer hours per night; in production-focused industries more than 44% of workers, such as factory workers and plant operators, were getting seven or fewer hours of sleep per night.

At some point in my career, I thought the more sleep-deprived you were the more productive you were. I would boast that I slept only three or four hours the previous night! Much later, I found I had been doing myself a big disservice. For sure, at some points, one may need to burn the midnight oil, but when this becomes a routine part of our lives, we're doing more harm than good to the brain. Our brains need sleep as a restorative offering to our brain cells, and to prevent stress and depression.

2. The brain needs a healthy sociable environment

Social interactions trigger the production of grey matter and healthier brain cells. Healthy interactions include spending quality time with family, schoolmates, and friends. Consistent or extended periods of isolation are not well received by the brain.

3. The brain needs to be involved in new things

New experiences unlock your brain cells. Discoveries induce more adaptive learning by establishing key brain circuits and enhancing one's capacity to insert new neurological frameworks that house these discoveries, adventures, and tasks.

A study from researchers at the University of Miami and New York University revealed that humans, just like lab rats, seem happier when they're exposed to novel experiences. We 'excite' our brain cells with novel experiences.

THE BRAIN NEEDS

... TO SLEEP

... TO SOCIALIZE

... TO INNOVATE AND TRY OUT NEW THINGS

Ideation: A byproduct of an efficient brain

I had always thought the spark needed to induce innovation came from creating the environment that would allow our mental creativity to thrive. Maybe this explains why we do better after we sleep on a problem or take a walk to clear our minds. After storing and processing millions of *info bytes*, our mental powerhouse needs to synthesize this knowledge into a neural circuit that generates innovation. But interestingly, the right conditions and state of mind that facilitate innovation may comprise procrastination and inactivity. From the outside it might look like downtime, but on the inside, our neurons are creating magic!

Studies have shown that when ideation creation occurs in our brains, brain cells generate several hundreds of milliseconds of gamma activity as neurons are connected in a new circuit of neural activity.

The brain can align numerous pieces of information across multiple historical moments. These pieces are coordinated when the brain collates and aligns information, generating electrical impulses and building circuits of neural activity. These new connections give birth to the ideation or innovation flash!

Eyes on the prize

Focus is an over-flogged term used everywhere: in orga-nizations, to redirect employees to stay close to com-pany priorities; in sports, to inform athletes to remain unrelenting; in school, to avoid distractions, and so on. In all cases, the message remains the same: keep your eyes on the prize.

It would be usual practice to learn focus from Bill Gates or academic authorities such as Carol Dweck, or busi-ness tycoons such as Satya Nadella of Microsoft or Sundar Pichai of Alphabet. Learning focus from one who struggled for years with his inability to focus, due to severe impairment in childhood, seems like asking for directions from a blind person. But this case is an exception.

Without a doubt, Michael Phelps is the most decked-up Olympian in history. He has an unbelievable 28 Olympic medals to his credit, including 23 gold, three silver, and two bronze. His 28 Olympic medals are head and shoul-ders above the next closest individual, former Soviet Union gymnast Larisa Latynina, with 18 medals. Phelps' 23 golds medals are 14 more than the nine each achieved by Finnish distance runner Latynina Paavo Nurmi, U.S. sprinter Carl Lewis, and swimmer Mark Spitz.

Phelps appeared in a total of five Olympics, making his premiere in the 2000 summer games in Sydney at the tender age of 15. In the following Olympics held in Athens, Phelps seized eight medals, six gold and two silver, while still in his teens.

But interestingly, Michael Phelps wasn't a superstar from day one. As a child, he was diagnosed with severe Attention-Deficit/Hyperactivity Disorder (ADHD). But, somehow, the very thing that should have killed Phelps' focus and held him back was the very thing that unlocked his unparalleled focus.

At the beginning

In his early school days, Phelps had problems with focus, and one of his teachers explained to his mother, 'Your son will never be able to focus on anything.' In *Beneath the Surface,* Phelps explains 'I simply couldn't sit still, because it was difficult for me to focus on one thing at a time... I had to be in the middle of everything.' Things went further south following his parents' divorce when he was nine; he was also victimized by bullying. Being diagnosed with ADHD compounded his already serious problems.

His first encounter with swimming

Phelps' mother decided to get him swimming at the same local aquatic club as his two older sisters, but it was a real struggle for him at the beginning. However, with practice, Phelps embraced his newfound love, and while his ADHD left him restless in class, somehow he could stay more focused when he swam. He would swim for hours and hours after school each day.

By the time Phelps turned ten, he was swimming nationally, and one year later, he was introduced to coach, Bob Bowman. Bowman would go on to expose Phelps to the most rigorous training sessions ever.

When the rubber did hit the road!

Bob Bowman admitted that the moment he met Phelps, he knew immediately that he had discovered that once-in-a-lifetime swimmer every coach dreams about. According to Bowman, 'He was so fast he had to swim with older swimmers and because I was a new coach and I wanted to impress them and think I was tough, I gave them an extremely difficult training program.

'Because Michael was the youngest, he would go to the back of the line...but by the end of the practice, and at the most difficult part of the training session, I saw a little cap moving up forward to the front of the line with each repeat swim. It was so remarkable, I'd never seen anything like it and when I went home that night I couldn't sleep I was so excited, but of course, I didn't tell him that.'

Bowman then had to raise the bar on his coaching skills to accelerate Phelps' improvements and continue to bring out the best in him. He dialed up Phelps' training workload and Phelps thrived with each new task. 'When I disciplined him and tried to get him to stop playing around I said, "you should be very tired, that's the hardest practice you've ever done." I'll never forget, he looked me straight in the eye and said, "I don't get tired"!'

In the first year that Bowman started training Phelps in North Baltimore, he asked him to pick his three favorite races, nominate the times he wanted to achieve for each, and make that his goal for the year. Phelps was exposed to rigorous training to prepare him for the toughest challenges ahead. Before Beijing, Phelps swam 21 races in three days and when he got to Beijing, he swam 17 races in nine days to secure his eight Olympic gold medals. Phelps' rigorous training ensured he was more than three times over-prepared for Olympic success.

The overriding principle that governed Phelps' amazing performances was that Bowman set up steep obstacles during his training to prepare him for the worst: 'I've always tried to find ways to give him adversity in either meets or practice and have him overcome it,' Bowman said. 'The higher the level of pressure the better Michael performs. As expectations rise he becomes more relaxed... That's what makes him the greatest.' No wonder Phelps titles his second book *No Limits: The Will to Succeed.*

A PICTURE OF PHELP AND BOWMAN

Agility to evolve where necessary

Once we activate a lifestyle shift, we also need to establish a system enabling us to continually implement other necessary shifts when and where we need to. How do we do that?

- Stay true to yourself. Whether it's identifying the right energy bursts, the cycle that works for you, or the most effective schedule and types of food...you must stay original.
- Find a benchmark achiever at each stage you would like to reach and use that person as a focal point. It's usually easier to prop yourself up when you have someone ahead of you who you can look up to. First, they show you that it's doable and, second, they inspire you to continually aspire.
- Learn to moderate between deliberate practice and flow. Angela Duckworth talks about deliberate practice as the key to deep practice, which is the one proven way to continually raise the bar on our performance. Flow can be likened to operating at mastery level. To achieve healthy improvement, one must cycle between deliberate practice and flow.

We are our habits and our habits are us! This is evident in the elements we have examined that enable us to disrupt our lifestyles to deliver excellence in any endeavor we pursue. We need to refocus our minds on energy management to enjoy high-level efficiencies in the workplace or our personal space. We also need to review our exercise habits and food composition and raise the bar on focus to hit the right results.

What did we learn?

We got to understand that Time Management is a fundamental expectation that must be complemented with Energy Management to achieve and sustain high levels of performance.

We went down the rabbit hole of the energy cycle and explored the key components of productivity – that being activity per time but amplified by leverage.

We also uncovered the pivotal role of food in our journey towards productivity. We looked at this from different viewpoints: the type of food and the circumstances around its consumption.

The maintenance cycle was also explored. We saw the positive impact an active lifestyle has on our health and overall performance. We discovered that we can improve our brain power and ensure optimal brain performance if we get the right amount of sleep to recharge, pursue social activities to trigger healthier brain cells, and seek discoveries that can activate the creative capabilities of the brain.

What's next?

To help reinforce the knowledge gathered so far in this chapter, on the next page you'll learn how to leverage a concept called *Managing your Cup of TEA* (Time, Energy, and Attitude). This is a robust concept that will enable you to:

1. Focus on the hybrid benefits of managing your time *and* your energy with the right attitude.
2. Put together a solid recipe to maintain the right lifestyle shift and stay dynamic to navigate hurdles as they arise.

Once we have successfully disrupted our lifestyle, positively and sustainably, we then need to take this mainstream by building momentum. We'll discover how in the final chapter.

Exercise: Managing your cup of TEA

Walk through the various sub-elements under each of the Time, Energy, and Attitude components (the TEA Concept) and run a self-assessment to see your opportunities and strengths – and how you can further raise the bar on your output.

Life Style Shift: Manage your Cup of Tea

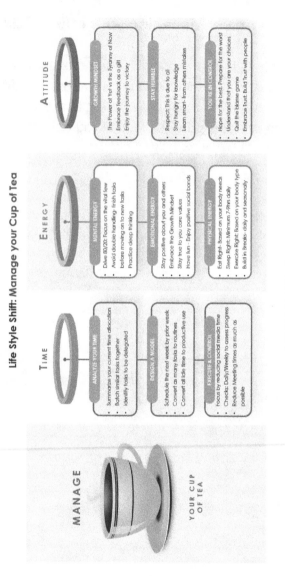

MANAGE

YOUR CUP OF TEA

TIME

ANALYZE YOUR TIME
- Summarize your current time allocation
- Batch similar tasks together
- Identify tasks to be delegated

DESIGN A MODEL
- Schedule the next week by prior week
- Convert as many tasks to routines
- Convert all idle time to productive use

EXECUTE & CONTROL
- Focus by reducing social media time
- Checks: Daily/Weekly to assess progress
- Reduce Meeting times as much as possible

ENERGY

MENTAL ENERGY
- Drive 80/20: Focus on the vital few
- Avoid double handling: finish tasks before moving on to new tasks
- Practice deep thinking

EMOTIONAL ENERGY
- Stay positive about you and others
- Embrace the Growth Mindset
- Stay true to you core values
- Have fun - Enjoy positive social bonds

PHYSICAL ENERGY
- Eat Right: Based on your body needs
- Sleep Right: Minimum 7-9hrs daily
- Exercise Right: Based on your body type
- Build in Breaks- daily and seasonally

ATTITUDE

GROWTH MINDSET
- The Power of Yet vs the Tyranny of Now
- Embrace feedback as a gift
- Enjoy the journey to victory

STAY HUMBLE
- Respect: This is due to all
- Stay hungry for knowledge
- Learn smart- from others mistakes

YOU'RE IN CONTROL
- Hope for the best. Prepare for the worst
- Understand that you are your choices
- Quit the blame game
- Embrace Trust: Build Trust with people

LIFE STYLE SHIFT DIAGRAM.

CHAPTER 7

Momentum –
The Winning Mindset

*'Our future is only limited by
our commitment to keep
the momentum going...'*

— Anne Sweeney

Keep Moving Forward

All knowledge remains only that until it is transitioned into practice. This is when we turn potential energy into kinetic energy, and once it is in motion, the question becomes, how can we sustain this motion? Here, it's all about *consistency over intensity*. James Rollins said, 'I'm pretty disciplined to keep the momentum of a story going by writing every day, even if it's only a couple of paragraphs or a page or two.'

This chapter will offer you a different view of success. A key priority will be seeing success as progress over time vs. seeing success as a point in time. You will learn to decouple momentum, reapplying the basic principles of momentum as we know them in the physical sciences. You will further observe the importance of the 'Power of *and*' alongside the synergies you can achieve by scaling up capabilities in a complementary manner. Finally, you will explore the pivotal role of execution with excellence as the one thing that moves the needle.

What is momentum?

Understanding momentum is the key to unlocking the mystery surrounding the highest levels of productivity in career, business, relationships, and family. It explains the forces that support a successful journey to achieving our goals.

We hear about momentum in diverse fields of knowledge. To the student of physics, momentum is the product of an object's mass and its velocity. In simple terms, momentum is mass in motion. For momentum to increase or decrease, there must be a corresponding change in either mass or velocity. We will represent this according to Newton's second law of motion as below:

Momentum (P) = Mass (M) x Velocity (V)

While this is a critical concept in physics, it is also analogous to the psychology and experience of momentum in human action. This analogy is often overlooked and under-used as a compelling force to reckon with.

Momentum describes movement, but not random movement. Momentum describes aligned movement. In the physical sciences, we define movement as *scalar*, meaning gaining distance, or *vector*, meaning attaining displacement. The difference between distance and displacement is that the distance may be random but displacement is aligned or defined with a given direction. In the same way, momentum is about movement that is aligned with direction. It is movement that is channeled and directed towards pre-set objectives, rather than random movement.

Components of momentum

Momentum involves both mass and velocity, and momentum is greater when either mass or its velocity increases. By mass, we mean some form of potential. When we think about moving towards success, our potential can be increased by gaining more knowledge, but it can also be decreased by losing knowledge. Yes, it's possible to decrease knowledge. Think about a time you learned something amazing but never implemented this knowledge. The odds are that over time this knowledge dwindled.

We can consider *momentum in practice* to be the product of our knowledge base and practice (the doing/verb form of practice) in terms of acquired skill. So, our equation on *momentum in practice* replicating the principles of Newton's second law of motion, $P=MV$, will become:

Momentum (P) = Knowledge base (M) x Practice (V)

This means we can increase our momentum through either gaining knowledge or increasing practice. Similarly, momentum can be built on more easily once we have begun improving both knowledge and practice (deliberate practice in this case).

Why momentum?

Momentum is critical for the simple reason found in the saying, 'Rome wasn't built in a day.' It takes baby steps to turn a toddler into a child and drops to make a mighty ocean. However, even though Rome wasn't built in a day, it was indeed eventually built! The key thing is that the journey should have a timeline for completion. Otherwise, it becomes a never-ending journey with no destination in sight.

This is the premise upon which momentum is built. Momentum hinges on the process rather than just the outcome, the journey rather than just the destination, and progress toward our goals rather than only the point in time when we achieve them. While that point in time may give us direction, it's just an element in the entire equation.

Momentum vs. motivation

People frequently substitute motivation for momentum. You may have heard people say, 'I don't have the motivation to do it.' While at face value this seems correct, when we dig deeper it is not consistent. Motivation is the reason to execute something, but doing it requires movement or momentum (energy in motion).

Just start!

How do you activate momentum? Remember, we talked about momentum in the physical sciences to be the product of mass and velocity. Momentum (P) = Mass (M) x Velocity (V). In psychology, momentum is the product of one's knowledge-base and practice (deliberate practice): *Momentum (P) = Knowledge base (Kb) x Practice (V).* It is the rate of change of knowledge and deliberate practice that determines our rate of momentum toward achieving our goals. In practice, momentum is activated through small incremental changes over time – small incremental improvements in either our knowledge base or deliberate practice.

One guaranteed way to ensure we maintain momentum is to constantly aim to achieve greater heights or goals, stretching ourselves to rise above new challenges. The brain expands with new challenges. Scientists discovered decades ago that the brain expands when we learn something new or embrace new challenges and shrinks when we repeat what we already know.

Momentum triggers a virtuous cycle of radical improvements

Momentum itself can induce a virtuous cycle of radical improvements. Consider how the brain develops intelligence. In the past, intelligence was assumed to be a function of intrinsic capacities, something you were born with. Stanford professor Carol Dweck tagged this idea the *fixed mindset* based on the thinking that our abilities are fixed or cast in stone and cannot be changed: if you're a smart individual then, no matter what, you will remain a smart individual. Nothing can change that.

However, research has shown the opposite is true: intelligence can be increased through incremental time and effort. Carol Dweck called this understanding a *growth mindset:* the understanding that intelligence and ability are not fixed over time but can grow.

It's easy to relate this to physical development, whereby muscles can be developed based on the rigor and amount of exercise engaged in. When strain is exerted on muscles over time, they expand and can endure more strain. At first, lifting a 20kg bar five times may feel impossible. But after the tenth try, it feels easier, and in a few weeks, you can lift 25kg or even 30kg, because your muscles have expanded.

The same rationale applies when a child tries a jigsaw puzzle. At first, it may look daunting, but with each effort, the child develops more skills and finds the puzzles easier. Now, the puzzle doesn't become any easier. Rather, the kid has become more skilled with effort and consistent practice. This is the theory behind 'continuous improvement' now trademarked as *Kaizen.* Kaizen is a Japanese philosophy first conceived during World War II as a radical way of thinking to incentivize continuous improvement in production.

> *'Persistence, perseverance, and continuous improvement are the ingredients for forming a successful person.'*

> — Debasish Mridha

The Kaizen philosophy of continuous improvement has been developed into a proven methodology that has been applied not just in production processes and systems, but in our everyday lives. Kaizen enables us to create the habit of achieving our personal goals and aspirations through a cycle of continuous learning, leading to growth and development. The learning process is holistic and comprises *learning, unlearning, and relearning.*

Your brain sees momentum as success

These signals are interpreted by your brain as success because it begins to view each small incremental improvement, rather than the overall delivery of the objective or attainment, as success. Momentum then triggers a snowballing impact that feeds off the accumulation of 'substance' during the journey. In this way, momentum begets momentum.

Often, people view performance and success as clearly linked, or identical. For a long time, I took this view and expected success to follow from performance. My understanding got a lot richer after I listened to Albert-Laszlo Barabasi's relatable explanation of the difference between performance and success. Usually, performance is the cumulative output of our activities.. We can measure performance using a clear standard. For example, you can gauge your daily walk steps against a target of 3000 steps a day. Or you can measure output in a race by how fast you swim 25 meters, or in a production line by how long it takes to produce 100 toilet rolls.

Sustaining momentum

To build momentum, we must be crystal clear about the journey and what it entails; we must plan to succeed, focus on the biggest priorities, learn from others, and execute with excellence. Building momentum could be the difference between a success story and a failure. The thin line separating success and failure involves:

- Clarity of vision: if you can achieve it in your mind, you will achieve it in due time.
- Articulating your vision into a mission and then your commission.
- Holding strong to your values.
- Working hard and smart – together.

Our goals constitute an articulated breakdown of our vision. Our goals are actionable parts of our vision and give life to it. As humans, we are goal-seeking organisms. We only function optimally when we work with clear expectations or objectives, and the fulfillment of a goal gives immeasurable happiness. If you don't have clear and specific goals in your life, you're doomed to work for people who do, and yet only 5% of people have articulated goals.

Write out your goals – all goals need to be in writing. Follow these steps to write down your goals:

- Every morning, rewrite your goals in the first-person singular, as though you have already achieved them.
- Every evening, review your progress, calling out what you did well or badly.
- Identify what you did right and what you would do differently if you had the day again.

By following this process over and over again you are programming your mind and creating habits.

Reviewing your progress swings both ways, including both the good and the bad. There's a lesson to learn in every setback. A critical aspect of project management is using the *lessons learned* file from similar projects. You must learn to identify the established principles from every event and in this way 'project manage' your goals.

'Wisdom is an equal measure of experience and reflection.'

— Aristotle

Momentum requires decisiveness

The reason most people are indecisive is that they're reluctant to make mistakes. Unfortunately, when this becomes a habit, it can condemn us to failure. The key is to make decisions and make them readily. It's easy to make decisions when you are clear about what you want, and that's why most people are unable to make decisions – because they don't have clarity. Without clarity, making a decision is like coming to a crossroads and not knowing which way to go next. About 80% of decisions should be made the first time they come up: simply make a decision; if it doesn't work, make another. If it still doesn't work, then you may be in the wrong field and should explore going back to the drawing board! Decision-making will help you gather momentum. The difference between achieving success and not achieving success doesn't necessarily hinge on making only the right decisions, but it may involve making decisions right!

Momentum requires capability building – study, study, study!

We need to constantly amass knowledge to become excellent at what we do. Knowledge can be learned from veterans in our chosen field through books, audiotapes, seminars, and direct work.

The habit of acquiring knowledge needs to be mainstream practice as we build momentum. In today's world, information is the most critical asset. If you read one book every week, you'll have read more than 50 books in a year, and your overall value will increase proportionately.

Tap into your creativity by feeding your curiosity. Ask questions like a child. All changes in our lives are most likely to come from taking in new information.

Momentum requires consistency over intensity.

A study was carried out in which CEOs were asked for the qualities they look for in top management staff. Their unanimous response pointed to 1) consistency in satisfactory job performance and 2) being dependable, predictable, and consistent. Satisfactory work will always be preferred above sporadic outbursts of brilliance or excellence.

Momentum requires focus

The ability to concentrate on one unique thing without distractions is integral to success. Focusing requires a high blend of accuracy and precision. Accuracy and precision are often thought to be the same thing, but they are different. Accuracy refers to getting as close as possible to the pre-set target, while precision speaks to having all shots as close as possible to each other. Training ourselves to focus means striving for high levels of accuracy and precision to the task ahead. This is developed, again, via deliberate practice enhancing the necessary skill set.

Leverage your clear-cut goals along with the 80-20 principle to produce a list of priorities and drive your energies accordingly. There's never enough time to do everything but there's always enough time to do the important and necessary things. You will need to deploy time AND energy management skills as well as develop the ability to concentrate with willpower and discipline. Concentrated effort is a source of energy and enthusiasm, as it makes you feel great when you're working on something important rather than something irrelevant.

Momentum requires interdependence

When we were young, we were mostly dependent. As we grew older, we learned how to be independent. However, to attain appreciable levels of success we must sync dependence and independence to achieve *interdependence*. Our relationships with our fellow humans are strong indicators of how well and fast we will rise in our chosen fields. Your ability to transition from independent to interdependent is a salient feature on the road to success. What you sow in your relationships, you reap.

> *'I've learned that people will forget what you said, people will forget what you did, but people will never forget how you made them feel.'*

— Maya Angelou

The one way to build and sustain relationships with people is to establish trust. In *Leading at the Speed of Trust*, Stephen Covey outlines the economics of trust and how lack of trust can backfire; it becomes a trust 'tax' that leads to further costs by increasing resources used to validate one's authenticity. Lack of trust can also decelerate execution due to time being wasted in multiple checks.

Covey presented the basic execution equation:

Strategy x Execution = Results

He explained that this equation contains a latent variable: trust.

(Strategy x Execution) x Trust = Results

If we have trust, we will invariably achieve accelerated results. People remain the greatest assets; we need to maximize interdependence as a leveraging tool that provides a competitive advantage.

Momentum requires courage

Courage isn't a lack of fear, but an ability and willingness to master and manage your fears. Courageous people are those who can face and confront their fears.

> *'Do the thing you fear and the death of fear is certain.'*
>
> — Mark Twain

Fear disappears like smoke when you confront its root cause. One thing that cripples our courage is not failure but the fear of 'failure.' The fear of failure leads to self-defeat even before the event! This touches on the power of 'mental imagery.' To overcome this effect, we need to learn to embrace failure as a stepping stone. We need to plan to fail fast and early, and then pivot quickly absorbing the learning inherent in our 'failures' and pressing on with this additional knowledge.

Helen Keller said *'life is either a daring adventure or nothing at all.'* The tendency to seek security is the low road to failure. If you're not truly afraid at least two to three times a week, trembling when you go to sleep, if you're not falling on your face now and then...you're not pushing hard enough and are living within your potential. Successful people live on the edge of what they're capable of.

The true test of courage is to consistently persist when things get rough. To pick yourself up when you fall over and fire again. The key deliverable when we're faced with obstacles is to set up the drive to develop momentum. And momentum isn't possible unless you're struggling against the elements or obstacles in your path. Struggle with adversity goes hand in hand with great success.

Momentum requires you to be unstoppable.

Your actions are the true measure of what you believe. Behavioral psychology tells us that even if you don't feel the part, acting the part will generate the feelings that will 'set' you up for momentum. Remember, after all is said and done – you 'must act.' Nothing can substitute for the hard work that you need to combine with smart work.

The power of AND

I recall vividly a strategy teacher from my MBA who uncovered the power of AND leveraging innovative ways to complement resources and capabilities. This would not just affect core business management, core product offering, and corporate or competitive strategy; it was a way of life. This speaks to building relevant connections between the critical resources and capabilities required to deliver results such that everything you do builds on what has already been achieved. While this sounds basic, it may be deferred to a default execution of activities in silos.

We must seek to build leverage in all of these areas by combining them with the power of AND as much as possible. For example, how can you connect with sponsors as well as mentors in your career and your office? Sponsorship makes all the difference. Most people focus on finding mentors, but having sponsors will give unparalleled results. Your sponsors build on what can be achieved with mentors to give you wings.

When talking skillsets, you need to build complementary solutions. Like a Lego system, everything needs to be a building block that supports you to deliver on your goals. Let's say you intend to become a movie star. You go to acting school to gain some knowledge and then pick a buddy who is a bit ahead of you to show you the ropes. At the same time, you do some free coaching with a group that has asked for voluntary support. All the while, you ensure 80% of the movies you watch are those with lead characters you model. You're building an *Activity System* that is setting the stage for you to truly become a movie star for yourself, and time will be all that stands between you and excellence. Over time, you will feel increasingly empowered, and the law of attraction driven by synchronicity will deliver opportunities when you are prepared – it's fireworks!

The winning mindset

Everything begins and ends in the mind. The mind is the greatest design factory of all. This also means that we win or lose from our mindset and must position our minds toward the winning front even before we embark on our journey to success. A few things can help us build and sustain the winning mindset we need throughout our journey.

Stay disciplined

We all know the saying 'Discipline is what you will and not what you feel.' Discipline is painful at the onset but the moment you integrate it as a habit, you're on the way to turning it into a lifestyle.

As you attempt to maximize your abilities and simultaneously achieve your goals with momentum, there will be many distractions along the way. You will need to stick to the principles that have gotten you that far. Now, this doesn't mean you must do the same things over and over...no! With changing dynamics across all levels of human existence, you will also need to be flexible. So, your ways may need to change, but your winning principles will remain.

Your will to prepare should never diminish, regardless of your achievements. In this regard, you will agree that the greatest barrier to success is indeed success itself. You must never rest on your oars, or on your laurels, along the way. While we need to appreciate our achieve-ments and remain thankful, we must also be relentless!

Now that you're the champ, it's time to turn it up, train harder, and keep raising the bar. Your opponents are coming for you – and you must never forget it. But first consider them as worthy rivals and this as a healthy rivalry. Competition leads to innovation and, yes, you have much to learn from your competition. They will keep you fired up to elevate your performance. On top of that, the world is watching and waiting. Imagine that you just got an incentive-based sales job. Imagine, too, that what you earn is 100% performance-based. This means nothing is guaranteed at the end of the month and you must work hard to achieve as much as you can. The downside is that if you do nothing you get nothing – that's fair. But the upside is that you have no limits!

This is the same thinking that will serve you in the game of life – it's 100% performance-based. You could exceed your wildest imaginations, or you could end up with nothing. You are the captain of your ship!

Be humble and stay humble

The greatest enemy of tomorrow's success is today's success.

The better you get, the more people will begin to let you know about it, and that can lead to false bravado and a belief that you are invincible. To keep moving forward in your career or endeavors, you must learn to ignore the hype and push harder than ever before, while still respecting the people who have helped you get to where you are. Keep the channels of feedback open and embrace criticism to help you continually improve. Never stop learning, never stop yearning.

Keep making bigger goals

Jordan Burroughs is a remarkable athlete. A four-time Pan-American and US Open National Champion and a 2012 Olympic gold medalist, Jordan is considered to be one of the greatest freestyle wrestlers ever. He said:

If someone would have told me years ago that I would be an Olympic Champion, I couldn't have imagined my wrestling career being much better, but now here I am in pursuit of a second Olympic gold. As an athlete, it's crucial to have lofty goals, and an incentive to drive you to complete it. What's your why? Set exceptional targets that will take time, diligence, and a ton of hard work to accomplish, and then work toward them every single day. This purposeful pursuit is what makes wrestling great. Standing on top of the podium is a fleeting, five-minute ceremony, but the memories created chasing the dream and character built along the way last a lifetime.

Regardless of how hard you train, there comes a time where you have to execute the skills you've learned and be rewarded for your sacrifice. Execution is what makes you memorable. Remember the guy that trained like a madman but could never put it together in the actual competition? Me neither! As the figure of speech goes, 'The hay is in the barn.' The work is done, the hay has been cut, and your family is in the audience. Don't let fear hinder your abilities, it's time to create a legacy.

Execution is the only strategy
the customer sees

A friend of mine, Scott Clary, a super-smart guy who hosts the *Success Story* podcast, once shared an interesting analogy between doing nothing at all and doing something via making small consistent efforts:

Option #1: $(1.00)^{365} = 1.00$ ----- *Doing nothing at all*

vs.

Option #2: $(1.01)^{365} = 37.70$ ----- *Small consistent efforts [incremental 1%]*

Option #1 for sure means nothing will change and one will most likely continue to complain and gloom over inertia in progress. Only Option #2 guarantees that one's situation will get better.

Taking action doesn't magically mean that your life will get better, nor that you won't succumb to setbacks, failures, redirection, and disappointments. But one thing is for sure: taking action will always be the option that results in gradual and systematic progress. Taking action guarantees momentum!

Resilience

*'Our greatest glory is not in never falling,
but rising every time we fall.'*

— Confucius

Let's consider one of the most resilient people of our time, a famous innovator who changed the luminous world as we know it: I'm talking about Thomas Edison. According to Edison, 'Our greatest weakness lies in giving up. The most certain way to succeed is always to try just one more time,' and, 'If we did all the things we are capable of we would astound ourselves.'

Resilience is born out of ensuring our efforts are constantly refired until the goal is achieved or the task is accomplished. It is 'never giving up.' The proportion of people who persist to complete their tasks is far less than the proportion that gives up. Thomas Edison also famously said, 'Many of life's failures are people who did not realize how close they were to success when they gave up.'

The same principle of persistence features in Thomas Edison's well-known statement, 'I didn't fail 1000 times. The light bulb was an invention with 1000 steps.'

Momentum requires you to execute with excellence

Every man or woman I have studied who has achieved anything great has done so by committing themselves to become excellent in their field. After speaking with movers and shakers, I have concluded that excellence in execution is an indispensable prerequisite for success.

In today's highly competitive world, you don't stand a chance at matching the speed of the game or standing out from the crowd if you're not excellent at what you do...unless you win the lottery! The terrain is highly competitive and the market only pays for excellence.

Excellence is a journey rather than a destination. The enemies of excellence include complacency and satisfaction. Excellence in execution means doing your best at every opportunity and always striving to do better.

Remember what A.G. Lafley said, execution is the ONLY strategy the customer sees. What he meant was that all of the background work, ideation, conceptualization, and design that goes into retail or consumer goods comes to nothing without the right execution.

After arriving at clarity of purpose with the right connections in place, we go back to ground zero if we don't drive consistent execution.

Focus on the process, not the outcome

The most sustainable way to drive consistency is by focusing on the process rather than the outcome. This stems from the fact that rather than setting goals we should achieve them by building momentum. In project management, we talk about *quality assurance* as the part of quality management that focuses on confidence that quality requirements will be fulfilled. Quality assurance is all about qualifying the process to ensure that the outcome is quality compliant. In the same vein, once we fix the process, the outcome invariably comes through, as the outcome is indeed an output of the process.

Renowned Harvard Psychologist Amy Cuddy said that the average person is likely to find more success if they shoot for 'just down the block' instead of shooting for the moon. We need to focus more on the process than the outcome. Again, you most certainly cannot lose 10kg overnight. Your best option is to divide your ultimate goal into a series of daily or weekly goals that are achievable.

According to Cuddy, 'lots of research is showing us that we do much better when we focus on incremental change, on little bits of improvement.' This is the way our minds interpret success. James Clear, the *New York Times* best-selling author of *Atomic Habits*, proposed that this is also how we create systems that set us up for success. He said that 'Every Olympian wants to win a gold medal. Every candidate wants to get the job. But if successful and unsuccessful people share the same goals, then the goal cannot be what differentiates the winners from the losers.'

Be bold: You have nothing to lose but everything to gain

Only a few people must have truly believed the words of President Kennedy on May 25, 1961, when he declared to the American Congress and, by extension, the world, that the U.S. would plant a flag on the surface of the moon. Looking at things pragmatically, the doubters may have had good reason at the time, as the U.S. didn't yet have the capability to launch or sustain such a project.

PRESIDENT JOHN F. KENNEDY ON MAY 25, 1961, DECLARED TO THE U.S. CONGRESS THE GOAL OF LANDING A MAN ON THE MOON BY THE END OF THE DECADE.

'...I believe that this nation should commit itself to achieving the goal, before this decade is out, of landing a man on the moon and returning him safely to the Earth. No single space project...will be more exciting, or more

*impressive to mankind, or more
important...and none will be so
difficult or expensive to accomplish...'*

— President John F. Kennedy, May 1961

And yet, yes! On July 20th, 1969, Kennedy's promise was delivered. We need to be bold and explore the unthinkable – as long as you truly believe, the world will be your oyster!

We have seen that momentum is the key to unlocking the highest levels of productivity and ensuring we keep progressing on the journey to achieving our goals. We broke momentum into its components and showed why momentum is perceived as success by our senses. We also explored how to sustain momentum when we embrace the winning mindset. We saw how this drives focus on the quality of execution to achieve incremental wins on our journey to achieving our ultimate goals.

Going forward: Maintaining the momentum mindset

To maintain the momentum mindset, we can implement a variety of controls to ensure we stay focused on driving continuous improvement:

1. Assess your progress based on the 1% incremental achievement baseline.
2. Convert all deliverables into smaller, actionable mini-projects.
3. Track, track, track: ensure progress is radically, and brutally, tracked.
4. Collate feedback to ensure continuous improvement from your customers'/stakeholders' perspectives.

There are a few further things that we need to do to maintain momentum:

1. Always consider yourself to be truly *unstoppable*. Barriers will arise, but once you determine in your mind that you're unstoppable, then you will think through solutions to overcome those barriers. Also, remember that these obstacles are temporary and can be overcome.
2. Always position yourself in the winning light. In marketing, one of the biggest drivers of value is perception. This comes from the way we position ourselves. First, position yourself to drive the right perception, and then showcase it via presentation.
3. Create your future (predict it).
4. Celebrate small wins – these drive momentum and accountability. Small wins are still wins.

    Celebrate with the team and set yourselves up for the next level.

5. Value *consistency* over *intensity*.
6. Focus on the vital few vs. the trivial many: remember the 80-20 principle.
7. Never stop yearning, never stop learning, so you won't stop earning!
8. Earn and spend the trust currency.
9. The secret to living is giving – live AND leave your legacy.

Momentum begins with you moving

At the end of the day, you need to stay true to yourself. You are the first and best measure of your momentum. You will know how and when you're making progress throughout the journey. Your conviction in your progress is critical as it generates the self-confidence that will further fuel the engine to keep progressing. You need to make that move, take that first step, and the journey will get easier the more you maintain your momentum.

The diagram on the next page will help you to visualize some of the critical elements you need to execute your mental designs into pure excellence. You may use it as a checklist or as a 360-degree feedback loop from purpose to execution, to controls and continuous improvement.

What did we learn?

We were able to observe success in a different light. Our mental faculties can be trained to rethink success as progress over time vs. achievement at a point in time.

We decoupled momentum, reapplying the basic principles of momentum as we know them in the physical sciences [Mass x Velocity] to reality – giving us momentum as a product of knowledge and practice to come through as [Knowledge x Skill].

We further explored the power of AND, understanding how we can build synergies by complementing capabilities, like a Lego system to achieve our competitive advantage.

Finally, we understood that regardless of all our daunting designs, remarkable plans, and game-changing strategies, if we don't' execute them, they will remain as designs, plans and strategies! We must build a system to execute, but also rely on feedback to continuously improve our activity systems.

What's next?

To ensure we make the move into momentum and deliver excellence in execution, see the Continuous Improvement Wheel on the next page. This shows a recommended approach to executing with excellence behind your established momentum. Consider this as an iterative process with no hard and fast rules.

We have gone through seven insightful chapters on practical systems to enable us to transition from goal to goal achievement. We now need to take stock of what we have learned so far, emphasizing the key themes, and ensuring we extract the most critical points to hit the ground running! We will do that in the concluding part of the book.

Execute with Excellence- *Continuous Improvement Wheel*

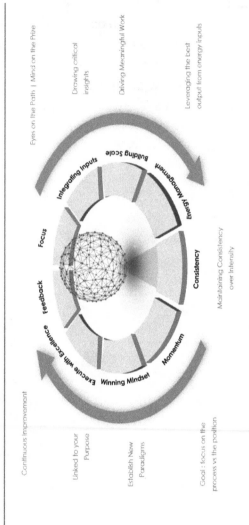

Eyes on the Path | Mind on the Prize

Drawing critical insights

Driving Meaningful Work

Leveraging the best output from energy inputs

Integrating Inputs

Building Scale

Focus

Energy Management

Consistency

Maintaining Consistency over Intensity

feedback

Execute with Excellence

Momentum

Winning Mindset

Continuous Improvement

Linked to your Purpose

Establish New Paradigms

Goal : focus on the process vs the position

ADAPTED FROM "3 STEPS TO ACHIEVING YOUR GOALS". SOURCE: IMOWO ENANG

Conclusion

s individuals, we all have ambitions and aspirations. But the difference between dreams or goals and their manifestation lies in the processes we follow to convert our dreams into reality, rather than simply wishing them into reality.

A proven model to help us transition from aspiration to seizing the fruits of our aspiration is disrupting our mindset and rethinking our methods to execute with pure excellence. It is vital to focus on the process and the journey as we achieve success one day at a time. Knowledge without execution is simply untapped energy. To hit the ground running, we need to transform this potential energy (i.e., what you have learned from this book) into kinetic energy (i.e., taking actionable steps in the right direction). I implore you to put these nuggets into deliberate practice at your own pace so that you can reap the benefits you deserve.

What's next? Take your time to leverage the tools provided in the templates and exercises in each chapter to build your route to excellence, aligned with your preferred timing – work out the best time to challenge your expectations and track your progress. Timing your progress may need to be a mix of what can be fit into your current schedule and what is challenging enough to act as a stretch goal. You may track your progress manually or using basic calendar apps (e.g., google calendar) and review your progress at specific milestones.

Above all, remind yourself day by day that success is made up of small incremental improvements, not necessarily big leaps. To truly enjoy the process is to build a sustainable pathway to success, and this can only be done by focusing on the process rather than the outcome.

Do reach out to share your progress with me along your journey to achieving your goals. I would like to hear from you if you have any questions or need further assistance. You may check out my website at imomazin.com or reach me on imo@imomazin.com or WhatsApp on +971 54 399 3100.

Further reading and resources

Introduction

Boyatzis, A., Smith, M.L., & Van Oosten, E. (2019). *Helping people change: Coaching with compassion for lifelong learning and growth.* Harvard Business Review Press.

Cambridge English Corpus. (2021). Mental imagery. In *Cambridge Dictionary.* https://dictionary.cambridge.org/example/english/mental-imagery

French, K. (2020, December 20). Why goal setting doesn't work. *Life Coach Directory.* https://www.lifecoach-directory.org.uk/memberarticles/why-goal-setting-doesnt-work

Big Picture

Canfield, J. (n.d.). Visualization techniques to affirm your desired outcomes: A step by step guide. *Jack Canfield: Maximizing Your Potential.* https://www.jack-canfield.com/blog/visualize-and-affirm-your-desired-outcomes-a-step-by-step-guide/

Carlyle, J. (2018, December 4). How writing down your goals will increase personal success tenfold. *Management 3.0.* https://management30.com/blog/writing-down-goals-for-success/

Clear, J. (2018). *Atomic habits: An easy & proven way to build good habits & break bad ones.* Random House.

Cuddy, A. (2015). *Presence: Bringing your boldest self to your biggest challenges.* Orion.

Gladwell, M. (2008). *Outliers: The story of success.* Little, Brown and Company.

Hargrave, S. J. (2016). *Mind Hacking: How to change your mind for good in 21 days.* Gallery Books.

Harrell, E. (2015, October 30). How the 1% performance improvements led to Olympic gold. *Harvard Business Review.* https://hbr.org/2015/10/how-1-performance-improvements-led-to-olympic-gold

Mansfield, S. (2018, December 9). The ultimate guide to marginal gains and the 1% principle. *CoachSME.* https://coachsme.co.uk/the-ultimate-guide-to-marginal-gains-and-the-1-principle/

Murphy, P. (n.d.). How to visualize something into reality: The process of creative visualization. *100 Years of Career Advice.* https://www.1000yearsofcareeradvice.com/how-to-visualize-something-into-reality/

Payne, I. (2019, September 12). How Bruce Lee outlined his plan to become America's first 'Oriental super star' – and earn US$10 million – in 1969. *South China Morning Post.* https://www.scmp.com/magazines/

style/news-trends/article/3026844/how-bruce-lees-1969-handwritten-plan-be-highest-paid

Williams, A. (2015, July 8). 8 successful people who use the power of visualization. *Mind Body Green*. https://www.mindbodygreen.com/0-20630/8-successful-people-who-use-the-power-of-visualization.html

Clarity of Purpose

Dyer, W.W. (2004). *The power of intention: Learning to co-create your world your way.* Hay House.

Gladwell, M. (2008). *Outliers: The story of success.* Little, Brown and Company.

Moore, K. (2015, January 19). The great power of connecting passion with purpose. *Forbes*. https://www.forbes.com/sites/karlmoore/2015/01/19/the-great-power-of-connecting-passion-with-purpose/?sh=6948eea88784

Robbins, T. (n.d.). Giving Back. *Tony Robbins*. https://www.tonyrobbins.com/giving-back/

The Power of Mental Imagery

Achronim, M. (n.d.). Jacob's sheep: Genetics and epigenetics in the Torah. *Mayim Achronim: Uncovering the depths of Torah's Wisdom*. https://www.mayimachronim.com/jacobs-sheep-genetics-and-epigenetics-in-the-torah/

Haviz, R. (n.d.). Thoughts and perspectives to enrich your mind and improve your life. *Think Grow Prosper.* https://thinkgrowprosper.com/

Hicks, E., & Hicks, J. (2006). *The law of attraction: The basics of the teaching of Abraham.* Hay House, Inc.

Marshall, L. (2018, December 6). Your brain on imagination: It's a lot like the real thing, study shows. *University of Colorado Boulder Today.* https://www.colorado.edu/today/node/31511

Murphy, P. (n.d.). How to visualize something into reality: The process of creative visualization. *100 Years of Career Advice.* https://www.1000yearsofcareeradvice.com/how-to-visualize-something-into-reality/

Penn, R.A., & Hout, M.C. (2018, November 28). Making reality virtual: How VR "tricks" your brain. *Frontiers for Young Minds.* https://doi.org/10.3389/frym.2018.00062

Robbins, T. (1986). *Unlimited power: The new science of personal achievement.* Simon & Schuster.

The Power of Leverage: Leverage In | Leveraging Out

Lehrer, Jonah (2015, March 4). How fast is Usain Bolt? *Jonah Lehrer.* http://www.jonahlehrer.com/blog/2015/3/2/the-syncing-of-sprinters

Ideas & Inspiration. (2019, April 24.) *Synchronicity for life success | Dr. Phil Merry* [Video]. YouTube. https://www.youtube.com/watch?v=2YTZn_T9w24

Nieuwenburg, J. (n.d). Work smarter, not harder: The power of leverage. *W5 Coaching.* https://w5coaching.com/leverage-help-get-success-business/

Radin, D. (2006). *Entangled minds: Extrasensory experiences in a quantum reality.* Paraview Pocket Books.

Robbins, T. (n.d.). [Brief article on leverage]. *The Power of Leverage: Creating Lasting Change Skill Session* https://www.tonyrobbins.com/resources/pdfs/The-Power-of-Leverage.pdf

SimaFore & Strat-Wise. (2012). *Practical implementation of the 80-20 principle in business.*

Varlet, M., & Richardson, M.J. (2015) What would Usain Bolt's 100-meter sprint world record be without Tyson Gay? Unintentional interpersonal synchronization between the two sprinters. *Journal of Experimental Psychology: Human Perception and Performance, 41*(1), 36-41. https://doi.org/10.1037/a0038640

Lifestyle Shift

Abraham, A. (2018). *The neuroscience of creativity.* Cambridge University Press.

Carson, S. (2010). *Your creative brain: Seven steps to maximize imagination, productivity, and innovation in your life* Jossey-Bass.

Ratey, J.J., & Hagerman, E. (2008).*Spark: The revolutionary new science of exercise and the brain*. Little, Brown and Company.

Gomez-Pinilla, F. (2012, December 21). How does the brain use food as energy?. *BrainFacts.Org. https://www.brainfacts.org/ask-an-expert/how-does-the-brain-use-food-as-energy*

Phelps, M., & Abrahamson, A. (2008). *No limits: The will to succeed.* Simon & Schuster.

Phelps M., & Cazeneuve, B. (2004). *Beneath the surface: My story.* Sports Publishing.

Poirier-Leroy, O. (n.d.). Visualization for athletes: How to crush the competition and your Workouts. *YourWorkoutBook.* https://www.yourworkoutbook.com/visualization-for-athletes/

Building Momentum

Burroughs, J. (2015, December 28). It never gets easier, you just get better. *Jordan Burroughs.* https://www.jordanburroughs.com/blog/it-never-gets-easier-you-just-get-better

CPSIA information can be obtained
at www.ICGtesting.com
Printed in the USA
BVHW070615020222
627781BV00004B/261

9 781761 240225